a learning process for religious education

RICHARD REICHERT

PFLAUM PUBLISHING, DAYTON, OHIO 45439

To Sara, from whom I never stop learning

Also by the author
Self-Awareness Through Group Dynamics

The author and publisher wish to express their gratitude to Father David Kasperak and the staff of the Department of Education, Diocese of Green Bay, Wisconsin, for permission to use the material in the appendices, which first appeared in *The Green Bay Plan*, copyright 1971.

ISBN: 0-8278-0001-0
Library of Congress Catalog Card Number: 74-14308

Printed in the United States of America

iv

foreword

In a sense, the last thing we need now is another book on religious education. So, why another book? Certainly not to improve on what already has been said so well and so often. Certainly not to add some startling new insight that will revolutionize religious education.

The purpose of this book rather is to provide what may be the missing link: the framework that will help us use more effectively all the methods, techniques, and materials that already abound for programming and teaching religious education. As such, this book has value for the professional religious educator who is already widely read but who is looking for a tool to help him synthesize his knowledge and experience. It is valuable also for the beginner and the amateur, providing them with a framework into which they can place the ideas and techniques they will be learning. (In this sense, the book could be used as a teacher-training model.) Finally, because this book is written in "layman's" language, it can be read with profit by persons not directly involved in teaching but who nonetheless are responsible for providing religious education: pastors and parish councils, but especially parents. Regardless of the group to which the reader belongs, the central purpose of this book remains: to relate how a person learns with what we do or should do to foster his growth in faith.

Chapter One:
overview

Probably more thought, energy, and money have been spent on religious education in the last ten years than at any other time in the Church's history. The results have been encouraging; any religion teacher, either professional or volunteer, now has access to vast resources. New techniques abound. All kinds of aids, from audiovisuals to simulation games, are readily available. Packaged programs on virtually any topic of religious education have been developed.

Yet any teacher recently "in the trenches" knows that techniques, methods, and aids, no matter how creative, are not the whole answer. Of course, the teacher's own personality and especially his personal witness are essential to any religion program. But we

1

may assume reasonably that anyone seriously involved in religious education today has the capacity, or at least the desire, to be an effective witness. So we cannot blame poor motivation or desire for the lack of success. What, then, is the missing ingredient for successful teaching? Why does a new technique gain initial student interest and then just as quickly "turn them off?" What are we doing wrong?

I believe the answer is relatively simple. Somewhere along the line, we have failed to develop a framework, a model, a theory of the learning process that enables us to use these techniques effectively. If we can understand the learning process, the steps or stages that anyone goes through when he learns something, we will better know where to use the various techniques, aids, and methods.

Techniques and aids primarily are tools for helping a person through a particular step in the process. For example, discussion helps persons clarify and reflect on the possible impact of an experience. This supposes a previous experience, hopefully a common one. This also presumes that the experience had enough personal meaning that students would want to clarify its significance. So religious educators do not need more techniques and aids but a better understanding of the learning process. This will dictate how and when to use all present techniques and aids effectively.

The purpose of this book is to examine the learning process and then to investigate how and when the various teaching techniques can be used properly.

An understanding of the learning process also will clarify the interrelated roles of parent, parish, and catechist in the process of religious education. Parents and parish community must be involved in the religious education of the young; it is not solely or primarily the responsibility of the religious educator.

A proper understanding of the learning process not only will reinforce that belief, it also will demonstrate precisely what roles parents and parish have in the process and why their failure to assume these roles will doom to failure any religious education, even the most professional.

These two goals—a more effective use of aids and methods and a more precise understanding of the various roles in religious education—will not be reached in this book through the complicated analysis of a new esoteric theory. They will be reached, rather, simply by taking a new look at what already exists within the religious education structure of any parish or school. To put it another way, the thesis of this book is that every teacher and every parish already have the necessary resources to overcome many of the current difficulties in religious education. These pages will present a synthesis of these resources and a model for directing their use.

learning process

There is no such things as *the* learning process. Despite the work of great men like John Dewey and Jean Piaget, there still remain so many biological, psychological, and cultural variables that we may never be able to define totally all that takes place when a person learns. Hence the phrase "the learning process" should be qualified. What we are describing throughout this book is only *one* theory or working model of the learning process. Other more sophisticated theories exist. For our purposes, however, the simplified model presented here seems best suited: the described steps of learning are manageable, if not all-inclusive; they are within the experience of most readers; their application to the teaching of religion easily can be made even by the amateur teacher. Keeping in mind that this model is one among many, and that there are other elements that also influence a person's growth, our analysis of "the learning process" and its implications for the teaching of religion is valid and hopefully valuable. As was mentioned earlier, the learning process we will analyze is not some new or profound insight. It is, in fact, something already familiar to us, precisely because we have been involved in it all our lives, whenever we have learned anything. It is a common-sense model of the learning process.

Let us define, at the outset, how the word "learn" is being used here, making a distinction between knowing and learning. To know is to have intellectual awareness of a datum. To learn is to integrate that datum into a behavior pattern, to use the datum to influence and to shape decisions and actions. For example, I may *know* smoking is harmful to my health. But if I still smoke, I obviously have not *learned* that it is harmful. So the learning process involves undergoing not only a change in intellectual awareness but also in behavior. One further distinction: learning is also different from training or conditioning. Training or conditioning simply alters behavior without increasing intellectual insight or authentic awareness. For example, a two-year-old can be toilet-trained. Only later, however, will the child learn personal hygiene, becoming intellectually aware of the value of proper sanitation for himself and others, and consequently choose to direct his behavior according to that awareness.

Learning, then, is a process of increased intellectual awareness or insight that results in a change in how a person decides, values, or acts. As such, learning is much more than simply coming to know something. Learning is a profound event, a real change in a person's way of living.

The process that leads to such a change in a person has four stages or steps: 1-starting point, 2-significant experience, 3-reflection, and 4-assimilation. Let's take each of them in turn.

The starting point in any learning process is basically a person's present state, the sum total of all that he has learned in the past. In that sense, the starting point is a person's present value system, his conscious behavior patterns, the principles he uses in making a decision. However, the starting point includes two other essential elements that greatly influence his capacity to learn: his psychological readiness and his cultural milieu.

Some examples may clarify what I mean. A sixteen-year-old youth may have learned prejudice toward a particular race or class of people. But since he is sixteen, he is psychologically ready to begin to adopt a more idealistic view of life. Suppose, also, that he is away from his home environment where he originally learned his prejudice. We can say that although his starting point for learning is one of a particular prejudice, he is in a good position to learn an authentic sense of brotherhood and to change his behavior toward the prejudiced group. If, however, the same youth is still living at home, it may be very difficult for him to learn a different pattern of thinking and acting. We also can take the example of a six-year-old. Because of conscientious parents, he has learned the value of sharing within the family. At age six, he is psychologically ready to begin expanding his relationships beyond the family. Finally, by attending a good school he is placed in an environment that will not only reinforce his already acquired ability to share but also will provide an opportunity to expand it to persons outside the family.

These examples illustrate two things. The person's

starting point, that is, his actual ability to learn, is somewhat complex. Second, it is essential for the teacher to gain as much insight as possible into the person's starting point. This insures not only that his teaching goals are realistic but also that the teaching method is adapted to the needs of the student.

A teacher, especially with many students, can hardly have a personal awareness of each child's family background and past experiences. But, there are two things a teacher can and should know. Psychological readiness to learn is rather well defined and supported by research. This is where the work of men like Piaget or Erickson, at least in popularized form, is essential for the teacher. There are fairly accurate norms for judging when a child is ready to learn to read, to think abstractly, to express himself poetically. In the same way, religious educators can judge when a child is psychologically ready for learning a sense of sin or for making the commitment implied in Confirmation.

Fortunately, most good religion texts today are based on the psychological readiness of the child for a particular aspect of faith-life. In any case, the religion teacher must be sure he is aware of the norms of psychological readiness for the children he is teaching. Otherwise his efforts may fail because his teaching goals will be out of touch with the child's starting point.

Besides knowing psychological readiness, the teacher also can have a general feel for the cultural influences of the community where he is teaching. Granted, the family has the greatest cultural influence on the child. But often the family is the product of the community. An obvious example would be a teacher working with the poor in an inner-city ghetto. The cultural situation in this case would not be hard to recognize and to analyze. The same would be true if a person were teaching in an affluent suburb made up mostly of professional persons. The poor ghetto child obviously will have a different kind of cultural readiness for learning than the child raised in the suburb. However, it is not always easy—and is usually dangerous—to stereotype a cultural milieu. So a teacher will want to gain some real insight into the cultural background of the community if he hopes to truly understand his students' starting point for learning.

Assuming the teacher is somewhat aware of his students' starting point, the next step in the learning process is the significant experience. If a person is to truly learn, something must happen that jars him from his starting point, from home base, from his present stability. This "something" is the significant experience.

The adjective "significant" is crucial. Different levels of psychological readiness, and different backgrounds and environments, determine each person's starting point. And the starting point establishes how "significant" any experience will be. For example, how often have you seen a movie that touched you deeply only to hear your friend say "what a waste of money." Your starting points for experiencing the movie were different.

Often a significant experience is quite dramatic: a serious accident that brings us near death, the actual death of a loved one, falling in love for the first time, becoming a parent for the first time—or any time. Such experiences, by their very dynamism, force us to reevaluate our present pattern of thinking and acting both toward ourselves and others. They almost force us to learn.

A significant experience, however, need not be dramatic. A casual comment from a friend—like "Gee, you're getting fat"—may start us reevaluating our present eating and exercise habits. A book that moves us, a stirring movie, viewing a newscast on TV—each of these is a potentially significant experience. Any one of them may "force" us to reevaluate our present lifestyle.

In the same way, the significant experience may be something almost instantaneous, like the casual comment, or it may be something that develops gradually over several months or even years, like a period of time spent in the armed services. The total experience becomes significant and causes us to give a conscious new direction to our life.

Finally, it can be hard to isolate one significant experience from others. Often they occur in clusters and interact upon one another. In combination they become the influence that forces us to reevaluate and give new direction to our lives. For example, imagine going away from home to college for the first time. Many significant things happen simultaneously: new freedom, new friends, new responsibilities, new environment, new ideas. Over the freshman year this combination of experiences forces the young adult to reevaluate and make decisions about himself, his behavior, his relationships and responsibilities to others. He comes home a different person. He may have "learned" more out of the classroom than in it.

As an integral part of any learning process, the significant experience is any event or combination of events that makes a person aware of how he has been living and the options he has for the future. But it is more than just an intellectual awareness. It is also an emotional awareness; it includes a mandate. If an experience is truly significant, it will demand—or at least result in—a reevaluation of one's present way of life. If it is a truly significant experience, it will put the person so off balance that he is required to do some serious reflection before he once again acquires a sense of stability or wholeness. For example, to receive a job offer for about the same amount of pay and for doing what you already are doing is hardly significant; it can be easily ignored. However, to receive a job offer for much more salary but in a job you don't particularly like will demand some soul searching and a serious decision. Such an experience is significant. It evokes reflection and a decision that changes your life one way or another. It results in learning.

Reflection, then, becomes the next step in the learning process. It is the easiest to explain because it is basically what the term implies: thinking about, mulling over, wrestling with, weighing. It often, but not necessarily, implies counsel, seeking advice, doing some fact-gathering. Prayer is obviously an integral part of reflection, at least for the religious person. The purpose of reflection? It is simply to regain the equilibrium lost because of the significant experience. Reflection is the effort to put our house back in order, to regain our former stability or "cool." Put another way, reflection is the attempt to analyze the significance of our experience and the possibilities and demands it contains in terms of changing our former thinking patterns and behavior. It's asking the question "What is the real meaning of what has happened to me?"

Like the significant experience reflection can take place over a long period of time or in a matter of moments. It may be painful and heart-rending or joyful and spontaneous, an "Aha!" of sudden insight that bursts on us even while the significant experience still is taking place.

In any case, reflection will lead, in terms of the learning process, to a decision. The decision is either to continue our present lifestyle or to change it in some way, great or small. But whether the decision involves a reaffirmation or a change, it is still part of the learning process. For in either case, the decision implies a new awareness and conviction, a new enthusiasm and freedom (or dread).

The decision reached as a result of reflection always will remain in the realm of the person's free will. Any experience that predetermines the decision is not actually an experience but a manipulation, and the resulting decision is merely a reflex action. In such a case a person hasn't learned. He simply has been trained to respond. Thus, the learning process we are presenting precludes the concept of conditioning. In fact, the learning process very often involves freeing a person from various forms of conditioning to which he has been subjected.

In moving to the last step of the learning process, assimilation, let us imagine a youth who, having attended a retreat weekend that was a significant experience, is "forced" to reflect on his own life. After serious reflection and perhaps some counsel from friends, he decides to accept the values presented that weekend and to begin acting upon them. He then enters the final stage in the learning process, an attempt to integrate these new insights into his present lifestyle, and to eliminate certain other values and actions. Notice that we say "attempt." The final stage of the learning process is where the learning actually takes place. It is a trial-and-error stage, often filled with doubt or at least confusion, unfamiliarity, a sense of not yet being comfortable in this new mode of living. Like the significant experience and reflection, assimilation may be made quickly or it may take place over a long period of time. In either case, it is an initial attempt to "try out" the new insight in actual life.

The "trying out" period can take two forms. It may be a trying out based on inexperience and backed by a firm resolve, or it may be a trying out based on inexperience and lack of firm resolve. For example, a ten-year-old, because of a significant experience provided in school, decides to treat his baby sister more kindly. He doesn't lack resolve or a firm commitment. But he may be terribly awkward in carrying it out, at least for a while. That is one form of assimilation. On the other hand, a teenage boy, because of the significant experience of a retreat weekend, decides to break off with a girl with whom he had become too intimate. His decision, however, is still colored by strong emotional and physical attraction to the girl. His assimilation will have periods of doubt, hesitation, and confusion even as he goes about developing a pattern of life that keeps him away from the girl. Does this mean he really hasn't learned? No. Rather, the lesson he has to learn is more painful and difficult. In fact, he may never lose his attraction toward the girl. The real test of his having learned to respect her and/or himself is whether or not he avoids intimacy with her, regardless of his continuing feelings.

The four parts of the learning process—starting point, significant experience, reflection, and assimilation—easily can be borne out by personal experience. Reflect on anything you have really learned and on when you learned it. You probably will recall that you were ready for it; something happened that really made you think; you then thought about what it meant to you, and, finally, you attempted to live out your conclusion.

This analysis of the learning process has obvious implications for religious education. We need to know "where the students are" psychologically, culturally, actually (starting point). We need to be aware of and/or provide, experiences in their lives that meet their capacity to learn (significant experience). We need to help them reflect on their experiences (reflection). We need to support them and provide opportunities for them to integrate the results of their reflection into their lives (assimilation).

Starting point, significant experience, reflection, assimilation—they are our analysis of the learning process. The remaining chapters will attempt to examine each step in more depth and to show the practical implications of this process in religious education—not to revolutionize it but to give more direction and effectiveness to the things already being done.

Chapter Three:
starting point

There is always something marvelous in observing the gradual unfolding of the infant's capacities. As if on signal, the creeper suddenly discovers crawling. The crawling child gradually masters standing, then moving from place to place "holding on," and finally, as if on signal, "lets go" and sets out on his own.

Parents know there is little they can do to speed up this process. There seems to be an inner clock that signals to the child when he is ready for the next stage of his gradual mastery of his world. Of course, parents can facilitate the learning by their encouragement; they can remove obstacles, provide the first walking shoes, expand the area where the child can roam. But if the child isn't ready to crawl or to walk, no parental effort can do much to advance his growth. Sooner or later, he will reach his starting point.

What has all this to do with religious education? Very much. Just as the developing infant experiences stages of inner readiness for learning a particular skill, so the developing person will experience stages of inner readiness for learning the particular aspects of living a faith relationship. For example, the six-year-old is highly imaginative, spontaneous, open. He has a readiness for experiencing wonder, awe, reverence for God's creation. In the same way, the sixteen-year-old normally begins to experience a readiness and capacity for philosophical thinking; a healthy idealism begins to unfold within him. In both cases, these traits are starting points for learning to live a faith relationship.

If the teacher is not aware of the students' starting point, it is quite possible that even the most sincere efforts at religious education will fail. By ignoring the starting point, we risk offering a program of religious education that is out of touch with the inner needs and capacities of students. Such a program, if it doesn't actually hinder growth, at least will be unable to foster it. On the other hand, the religion teacher who knows the starting point of his students has insight into what will be "relevant" to them.

Relevance is not so much something outside the student, something novel, contemporary. Relevance is determined by the child's inner need, his inner readiness for a particular experience, insight, value, behavior. For example, the film *The Parable,* perhaps one of the better religious education films ever made, has not lost its relevance because it is no longer new. It is just as relevant today as when it was made, provided it is shown to persons who are at that point (starting point) in their maturing where its con-

16

tent can be experienced as relevant. The film never will be relevant for sixth graders. It always will have potential relevance for the young adult.

This knowledge of students also will help determine realistic goals for the year. Often, of course, a parish or school will select a textbook series, so goals are predetermined by the text. Most modern textbook series are based on the principles of psychological readiness, so their goals usually are realistic. However, as textbook publishers will admit—at least privately—certain concessions are made to those persons who find contemporary catechetics a scandal. Thus, certain topics and goals are introduced at various grade levels not so much because the students are ready for them but rather because some pastors, teachers, and parents would be nervous if the topic were not treated. In most current textbook series, you still can find an intellectual presentation of the Trinity introduced in the first or second grade. Even the most casual knowledge of psychological readiness tells us such a topic doesn't fit the need or capacity of that age group. So if a textbook is chosen for you, you will want to evaluate and adapt it to your students' starting point, being selective about what you present. On the other hand, if you actually are responsible for developing a program or curriculum, it becomes essential that you set your goals in relation to the starting point of each age group.

Knowledge of the students' starting point also will give valuable insight into the kinds of methods best suited for a particular age group. Discussion, for example, will be suited very well to the late adolescent because he is ready for serious conversation and needs opportunities to verbalize his thoughts and attitudes about faith. The sixth grader is much more action-prone than verbal—that is part of his readiness. Too often, however, religion reachers give in to a kind of faddism. A new method, like simulation or value clarification, is introduced; teachers at all grade levels attempt to utilize it, ignoring the fact that it really may not fit their students' readiness. After a few failures, the method is discarded as ineffective. Or worse, its usefulness is destroyed because, when it is introduced again, the students, though ready for it, react with "Oh, not that dumb thing again."

Closely involved with relevance, goal setting, and choice of methods is the whole question of motivation. We will spend more time on this topic in a later chapter, but it at least should be introduced here. Insofar as there is an inner readiness for certain kinds of experiences and learning, the readiness itself becomes the motivation for the students to learn. The ten-year-old doesn't need to be motivated to put logical order into his world; he wants to name things, to categorize them, to take them apart to see how they work. Such motivation comes from within. The alert teacher or the effective curriculum uses this momentum, this natural motivation, by providing related opportunities and challenges. While the question of motivation is more complex than this, the fact remains that the religion teacher can resolve a great deal of his problems of motivating students if he is aware of their starting point and adjusts his topics to it.

What are the elements that compose a person's starting point or readiness for religious education? Since the goal of religious education is *lived* faith or the fostering of a personal relationship with God, psychological readiness for religious education embraces the whole person: emotional, spiritual, and intellectual needs and capacities. However, each aspect is not equally important at each stage of the person's growth. For example, it is rightly said that religious education begins at birth. During those early months and years, the love and care provided by parents become the emotional foundation for the child's capacity to trust and to be open to others in later life—capacities essential to a faith relationship. During that same period, however, the child's spiritual and intellectual capacities are virtually dormant. Thus, religious education during the preschool years and early grades will center basically around emotional development. Only gradually are the spiritual and intellectual dimensions introduced in any formal way, as the child's starting point begins to dictate.

Does this mean that each teacher must attempt to analyze the emotional, spiritual, and intellectual starting point of his class? Yes and no. Yes, the teacher should become very familiar with the norms of psychological readiness for the age group with which he works. No, the teacher need not start from scratch to conduct personal research. To a large extent, the work of analyzing the child's and youth's readiness for religion at each stage of growth already has been done. It can be found in various books on developmental psychology, in various religious education curriculum guides, such as the NCEA study and the *Green Bay Plan,* and in teacher handbooks that accompany some textbook series. Most teachers already have a basic awareness of this information. Hopefully, it can be seen now as an integral part of successful religious education and a lot more sophisticated than such cliches as "Kids that age are self-conscious" or "Teenagers tend to be rebellious."

In deepening his knowledge of the students' starting point, the teacher must remember that their cultural environment to some degree can alter their natural readiness. A twelve-year-old in Southern California typically will display more worldly sophistication than a child the same age living in the rural Midwest. This fact as such is neither good nor bad. But it does mean the child from California will tend to ask questions, to be interested in topics, to experience a degree of confusion or uncertainty that will not characterize his peer in the Midwest. Even the better textbooks or curriculum guides cannot take this into account; it remains for the teacher to make whatever adjustments are necessary to insure that the goals, content, and methods are adapted to the starting point of the children in that environment.

A person working with children from an inner-city ghetto obviously would approach his students differently than a teacher working with children in an upperclass suburb. Not so obviously, the same need for adaption may be necessary within a single parish from year to year as the cultural environment changes. For example, a neighborhood and its population can change simply in the closing of a factory or by the introduction of a few high-rise apartments or a shopping center. To say this another way, next year's eighth graders won't be the same as this year's. While their starting point will remain basically the same and the goals may be basically valid, it usually will be necessary to make adjustments that reflect the subtle effects that the changing cultural environment has on the students' starting point.

Perhaps this all sounds too complex and impractical for the "working teacher," either professional or volunteer. But all it is saying is that the teacher must know his students. We simply are pointing out that a systematic approach to such knowledge is better than operating out of a few hunches, clichés, or intuitions. Moreover, the formulation of the starting point usually is more effective and accurate if it is done by teachers working together, pooling resources, insights, past experience. For the volunteer working in a CCD situation, it is assumed (perhaps naively) that he will get some assistance in understanding his students and in establishing his goals and methods from a master teacher, religion coordinator, or other professional catechist.

Accurate knowledge of the group's starting point will minimize the problem of individual differences; the goals and activities will be good for most of the students most of the time. When a student does not fit the typical characteristics, it is often quite evident. Most fourth graders, for example, are extroverted, adventuresome, eager to explore and discover. That's part of their starting point. The shy, retiring, passive child will tend to stand out immediately. On the other hand, most eighth and ninth grade boys will tend to be awkward and easily embarrassed in the presence of girls the same age (though just as often they try to disguise their discomfort with airs of indifference). A boy poised and at ease in that situation will be hard to miss.

With some imagination and initiative, those individual differences can be handled easily. For example, you simply wouldn't make the same demands to participate on the retiring fourth grader as you would on the rest of the class. On the other hand, you would want to give the poised ninth grader some chance to "perform," both to utilize his present capacity and to give some encouragement to his more awkward peers.

These are relatively simple examples of individual differences. Others, unfortunately, require more specialized treatment, which even may include counselling or special remedial work. (Yes, there is such a thing as remedial work in religious education.) The fact remains, however, that if the teacher is basically accurate in determining the starting point of the class as a whole, he will minimize the kinds of individual differences requiring his attention. He also will have a much better norm for determining which individual differences need attention and which ones will not interfere with reaching the goals set for the student.

In summary, the learning process begins with an inner dynamism or psychological readiness that we call the starting point. The teacher doesn't create this starting point, but he uses it to determine the goals and methods appropriate for his students and as a basis for motivating them. The starting point is also a means of evaluating existing texts and other aids. And while it remains basically the same for all children of a particular age group, the starting point can be altered by outside influences. While common-sense intuition and practical experience can provide some understanding of the starting point of students, a more sophisticated and accurate understanding will make the religious education program more effective. The program will be in touch with the students "where they are," something even our best efforts in the past have not always been able to guarantee. Included as an appendix to this book are a series of profiles of the starting point of students at various age levels. These were developed by the *Green Bay Plan*. While not definitive, they should provide a better feel for what is meant by an analysis of a student's readiness. The developmental chart included inside the covers of this book also should prove very practical.

Chapter Four:

significant experience

Suppose a person enrolled in a leadership training program only to find out that most of the program centered around sensitivity or encounter activities. While he may not have been ready for such an experience, it nevertheless happened to him, and it could have the ultimate effect of altering how he relates to others. Or, imagine a more familiar situation: falling in love and eventually marrying. While "falling in love" has some of the earmarks of a happening, it usually occurs because a person is ready for the experience and is open to it. This doesn't mean a man gets up one morning to decide to fall in love. It simply means that, over a period of time, he has developed a greater interest in women, is eager for personal relationships, and probably is dating regularly. When he does meet *the* girl, it is certainly a happy experience and not totally unexpected.

In both instances, it is obvious that the person learned, and learned in the fullest sense of that word. That is, he began to think, to judge, and to behave differently because of the experiences. In terms of the learning process itself, the examples illustrate two facts. First, learning—*all* learning—implies that a significant experience takes place. Second, though most experiences are significant for us only because of our readiness or openness for them, some experiences are significant on their own merits. They break in on us whether we are ready or not. What does all this mean?

In answering that question, we will cover several areas: we will situate and clarify the role of the significant experience in the overall learning process; we will discuss in detail what makes one experience significant while others remain insignificant; and we will make practical application of the principles we develop to the task of the religious educator.

The last chapter indicated that the starting point of the learning process is a given—though not necessarily one that is discerned easily. It is the person's present state of readiness, his own inner dynamism urging growth of a particular kind. But unless something happens outside the person to stimulate and channel the inner energy, it is possible for the person to stagnate. An extreme example might be those grotesque instances in which a perfectly normal child has been kept isolated from all social contact for a long period of time by a mentally sick parent or guardian. When discovered, the child is a virtual animal, with no ability to speak and in some instances even unable to move except on all fours. The other extreme would be an instance where a person has an experience so powerful that he is not yet ready to cope with it. This often results in neurosis or serious mental illness, as in the case of a child who witnesses the murder of his parents. Even the most mature are seldom ready to learn from such an experience.

Within the boundaries of these extremes lie an infinite variety of experiences that are the source of our learning. Significant experience may be anything from a casual remark to being held as a prisoner of war for several years. What makes the experience significant is its quality to move us, to stimulate us, to demand from us serious reflection and an eventual decision. Without such experiences we stagnate; with too many or the wrong kind of experiences we break.

An example may help demonstrate the essential role of the significant experience in the learning process. You have a vague uneasiness about whether you've sold out to the "establishment." You've gone materialistic! That's your starting point. A homily on Sunday, a newscast on Tuesday, a letter on Friday asking for a donation to a leper colony—any of these is a potentially significant experience demanding some kind of response in terms of your uneasiness about your present values and lifestyle. Each is an opportunity, maybe even an ultimatum, to grow, to learn. Suppose, on the other hand, that you slept through the homily, watched a quiz show instead of the newscast, or tossed the letter in the wastebasket unopened? Nothing significant happened, and you continue, maybe even become comfortable, in your situation.

Life—dare we say God—is constantly presenting significant experiences, each an opportunity or challenge to grow. Learning is stimulated, or rather provoked, by experiences that demand some reflection and decision. If you are deprived of such experiences, or if you shield yourself from them, learning is impossible. It is like putting off making an appointment with a doctor for fear of what he might tell you—a potential significant experience. So all learning depends upon experiences—*significant* experiences. That is the sense in which we can most accurately say: All learning is experiential.

What makes one experience significant and another insignificant? As the opening examples show, an experience is significant for one of two reasons. Either it is so powerful that it breaks in upon us "ready or not" and demands a response, or it is an experience for which we are psychologically ready. For example, it is doubtful that the Hebrews were ready for the experience of deliverance called Exodus. Yet it happened to them, and they had to deal with it. It demanded that they rethink and reevaluate their entire history. The result? They *learned* that Yahweh is a saving God. That *learning* reshaped their whole manner of living. It's equally doubtful that the Apostles were ready for Jesus' death, much less his Resurrection. Nevertheless, they experienced both. The result was the need to rethink, to reevaluate, and consequently to change their lifestyle, a change that resulted in the foundation of the Church.

These, of course, are examples of experiences so powerful that they demand a response regardless of readiness. In such cases, we learn despite ourselves—which is what revelation and gratuitous redemption probably are all about. More often, though, we learn precisely because we are *ready* for a particular experience. A conscientious mother, for example, constantly surrounds her child with books, games, and toys intended to help the child learn the alphabet. No one book, toy, or game is particularly significant, but when the child is *ready,* any one of these stimuli suddenly may become significant. Or, a mother may spend months trying to impress upon her teenage daughter the importance of grooming and neatness, all to no avail. Then *the* boy enters the girl's life. That experience, for which she is ready, puts into perspective all her mother has been saying. She suddenly becomes the epitome of feminine toilette and charm. Were the mother's efforts wasted? Certainly not. She created an environment that enabled the child to respond favorably *when* she had the significant experience. Note that the mother's efforts didn't provide the experience, but they did prepare the child to make the "right" response when an experience demanded she change her present style of living. One final example. A teacher, aware of the starting point of his ninth-grade students, provides them with an overnight in which they have plenty of opportunities to be together in a non-threatening situation. There are certain challenges or responsibilities they must meet—say, doing the cooking——and an opportunity for celebrating their "togetherness" in a liturgy. The teacher, at least potentially, has provided them with a significant experience, which triggers in the students the need for reflection, a consequent reevaluation of who they are, and ultimately a change in their behavior.

To sum up: We need experiences (stimuli) if we are to learn, that is, to grow. Most experiences stimulate growth or learning precisely because we are ready for them. Sometimes experiences burst in upon us "ready or not" and force us to learn. That, in brief, is the role of the significant experience in the learning process. Now we must consider what practical value this might have to the once-a-week catechist, the professional teacher, or a parish or diocesan director of religious education.

Since faith-life, the goal of religious education, embraces every dimension of the person, virtually any experience could initiate the process by which that person learns to live more faithfully. The whole world can be the religious education classroom. This should be both encouraging and humbling to the religion teacher—encouraging because it means religious education is potentially taking place all the time regardless of (sometimes in spite of) what takes place in religion class, humbling because the religion teacher is not the "whole show."

A second point is that no matter how carefully religious education is programmed in terms of the students' starting point or readiness, experiences can crash in to demand that the students' growth in faith take a whole new direction. A classic example is the conversion of St. Paul: a single experience changed the whole course of his faith-life. Examples closer to everyday experience would be such events as a flood or tornado, the sudden death of a classmate, word that a brother is missing in action, winning a state championship. In the face of such an unexpected significant experience, the teacher will want to put aside the curriculum to help the students form a faith-filled response to the situation.

Such unexpected significant experiences often can be interpreted as theological signs: human events bursting with God. A theological sign is God's way of revealing himself. It is his way of calling us to grow, to learn, to be more faith-full. It is an opportunity to become more than we are. For that reason, one of the more essential roles of the religion teacher is to be an interpreter of signs, a person who facilitates the students' response to God's call contained in these signs. (Isn't this the definition of a prophet?) As we will see shortly, the teacher often is involved in initiating the learning process by providing potentially significant experiences. But it is critical that he remain very sensitive to events in the lives of his students that in fact are signs from God. He will want to deal with these events before all others. Such events aren't always so obvious and dramatic as a tornado that wrecks half a town. Therefore, sensitivity to signs of God in our lives requires a habit of prayerfulness, something every serious religion teacher ought to pursue.

Every significant experience, of course, is not necessarily a sign of God, at least in the sense that we should look for some profound message akin to Paul's conversion experience. But it remains true that the teacher will want to stay very much in touch with the everyday events affecting the lives of students. Homecoming week, prom preparation, class elections—these are all potentially very significant to students, and they can initiate their need to reflect, to shift values, to change behavior. It is essential that the religion teacher not just "use" these experiences as interesting topics in class but actually attempt to bring the light of the Gospel to bear on them so that new values and behavior can be faith-full. Even such ordinary events as a class play, a candy drive, a school picnic can be opportunities to help students learn in practical ways what the Gospel means by cooperation, sharing, generosity. In short, most of what we can call significant experiences will take place *outside* the classroom.

One of the major tasks of the teacher will be to find ways of incorporating these significant experiences into his teaching. The student's experience may have been significant because it was powerful and unexpected, or simply because he was ready for it. In either case, the student's inner dynamism, his drive to grow and to learn, now is centered around that experience. It's what he is presently dealing with and what's taking up most of his emotional and intellectual energy. The curriculum, for example, calls for us to deal with moral responsibility. The topic is in keeping with the starting point of the age group, so we plan our lesson around it. However, we also should plan the lesson around what is presently significant in the lives of the students: the moral responsibility involved in loving another person, the moral responsibility involved in the way students treat the fans of the opposing team at the homecoming game, the moral responsibility involved in reporting a friend who is using drugs. The precise topic will depend on "what's happening." But the general topic can be planned well ahead of time.

By focusing on currently significant experiences and relating them to the topic suggested by the curriculum, we do two things. First, we utilize and channel the students' present drive to learn. They really need to make sense out of what is happening to them, to discover its potential meaning for them. They really want to grow. The power of every truly significant experience, even the least dramatic, is such that motivation is no problem provided the students can see the relationship between what we are doing and the needs they are experiencing. Second, assuming that the general topic is in keeping with the students' overall starting point, we also are utilizing the more general inner dynamism at work in students. The starting point tells generally what will be relevant, meaningful, necessary to the students. The particular significant experiences dictate a specific way to best approach the general topic. In this kind of planning, everything tends to work for the teacher because he is following the natural learning process.

At first, this may seem to place unrealistic demands on a teacher, especially a volunteer who has little contact with students outside the once-a-week meeting. How can he be expected to know what is really significant in the lives of his class? Obviously he can't know everything that is happening. But neither is he living in a vacuum. The newspaper and television can provide at least some general indication of what may be happening in the lives of students. He probably has friends with children the same age as those he teaches. Or perhaps he has children of his own. He certainly can find some time simply to talk with his students, to find out from them "what's happening." Again, I would assume (naively) that the volunteer receives some guidance and help from a master teacher or religion coordinator who is in touch with students. In any event, to ignore the significant experiences in the students' lives is a serious mistake, opening the door to the kind of criticism religion teachers have too long heard from students: "What's all this religion stuff got to do with me?"

While life itself provides students with many significant experiences, there are times when the religion teacher must create a potentially significant experience. How can this be done?

First, and in some ways most important, the teacher himself is a potentially significant experience. His manner of living, his convictions, the way he relates to the students—all can evoke in the students the need to reflect on their own lives, values, convictions, behavior. This is what is meant by "giving witness." It is why we can say a teacher teaches as much by who he is as by what he says. Such witness isn't something that can be programmed. Either it's there or it isn't. But we mention it to reinforce the idea that the religion teacher often is the best instrument God has for revealing himself. The religion teacher can be a sign. The religion teacher can be a significant experience to his students.

Besides himself, the teacher can provide significant experiences through life-oriented activities such as field trips, projects, encounter weekends. Visiting a home for the elderly is more significant than hearing a talk about the problems of the elderly. Undertaking a project to provide the elderly with a party will be more significant than a one-time visit. Note that such projects and field trips aren't just gimmicks to entertain students. They have a very serious purpose: to attempt to provide an experience so significant that the students will feel a need to reflect on it. Note too that the project or field trip is an initial step in the learning process. Unless it is followed by an opportunity to reflect on its meaning for their own faith-life, it can be considered a waste of time and an injustice to the students. Hence, the project or field trip must be planned in relation to some goal you hope to reach. Given these principles, all life-oriented activities are a valuable tool for the religion teacher, probably the best he has.

One step below these life-oriented experiences are structured experiences. These structured experiences include simulation games, group dynamic games, and such events as a "light show." Like life-oriented activities, these are governed by the principles mentioned above. The technique must suit the goal and must include an opportunity for reflection—assuming the activity triggers the need to reflect. More important, it must be suited to the readiness of the students. An activity demanding a lot of self-disclosure may be too threatening for a freshman and totally beyond a fifth grader; but it may be very effective with seniors. Too often a game is used only to fill time or because it is currently "in" even though it has no relation to the students' starting point. Instead of being a significant experience, the activity only succeeds in confusing or turning off students. For this reason, it often happens that a simulation or group-dynamics activity developed by the teacher himself will be more effective as a significant experience than a packaged game or an activity taken from a manual—not that these aren't valuable; but there is less chance of misusing such activities when they are "homemade." In developing the activity, the teacher is forced to think through his goal and to take into account the students' readiness for the experience.

Simulations or dynamics need not be limited to the confines of the classroom. One example is a "concerns scavenger hunt." This involves the students' going to a random selection of homes and asking residents to cut from the evening newspaper the article that most disturbed them. The purpose for such an activity and the object collected could vary depending on the particular goal of the class. In any event, the experience will tend to be more significant and to stimulate more discussion than an activity confined to the classroom. Because of their potential for providing students with significant experiences, simulations and related activities have won a central place in religious education; we no longer have to wait for "life" to provide all experiences. If used properly, these structured experiences will continue to be a valuable tool. If their function is misunderstood, however, they will become just another fad that sweeps through religion education, ending up on the shelf with our old collages and last year's overhead transparencies.

Besides life-oriented activities and simulated life activities, the teacher also can use some rather traditional methods of providing a significant experience. For example, Buscaglia's video-taped lectures on love have proven to be a very moving experience for older high school students and adults. Their power lies in the man himself and his message, an excellent proof that the spoken word and personal witness are still potentially as significant as any simulation a teacher can provide. A good talk, especially one that is a personal witness, or a well-chosen film, or the right book—all are still potentially significant experiences that the teacher should not overlook in his frantic search for the latest simulation game or the newest kind of service project. At the same time, the teacher will want to be very careful that these kinds of tools provide significant experiences. Because you like *The Velveteen Rabbit* or *Jonathan Livingston Seagull* or have found all kinds of religious meaning in *Black Orpheus* doesn't guarantee that students will be affected the same way. More than ever the teacher will want to be sure of his students' starting point.

The teacher faces another problem. Many students have formed so much prejudice toward such methods that it can be difficult to keep them interested long enough for the talk, film, or book to become significant to them. Generally, such audio and visual tools will be more effective with the younger students. Hearing a story can be a very significant experience for a third grader; so can viewing a film suited to his age. He is open to such experiences because of his lively imagination and his capacity to identify totally with what is happening. The older student becomes more analytical, and he develops an ability to remain detached from such experiences. For that reason, while the talk, film, and book still are valid tools for providing significant experiences, often they are more effectively used with older students in helping them reflect upon experiences they already have had. More about that in the next chapter.

In summary, we can say that all learning, including learning to live by faith, requires significant experiences that move us to reflect on our present life-style and to make decisions that affect our future behavior. Most of the experiences are found in life itself. In a real sense, they are the stuff of life. Some experiences burst in on us, moving us because of their very power; others are more predictable and affect us because we are psychologically ready to move on, to grow.

The religion teacher must be sensitive to the really significant experiences of his students. Those are the ones he will want to relate to the Gospel. Often, however, the teacher will find it necessary to provide a significant experience in order to stimulate such reflection. Besides his own personal witness, the teacher can have recourse to life-oriented activities like field trips, projects, liturgies, encounters, prayer services. If these are not possible or advisable, he can use simulations, group dynamics activities, and the like. He can use the more traditional methods such as a talk, a film, or a book. He can combine several approaches. Regardless of the method used, the teacher should be governed by certain basic principles. The method must suit his overall goal, coincide with the students' starting point, and include some opportunity for reflection. And out of this significant experience will come the next step in the learning process: reflection.

Chapter Five:
reflection

Each time a person has a significant experience, he will find it necessary to evaluate his present knowledge, values, and behavior in the light of that experience. This evaluation, with the eventual decision it implies, is the step in the learning process that we call reflection.

The time demanded for reflection will vary, depending on the nature of the experience and the implications it has for changing one's lifestyle. For example, after hearing a moving talk by a missionary, it may take little time to decide that his cause is worthy of your support. So you pledge a dollar a month. Though the decision does effect a change in your lifestyle, it does not bring about a big change. On the other hand, if the appeal were made for you to uproot your family to work in the mission fields, and you were deeply moved by the appeal, you then would be confronted with a decision that would take considerably more reflection. In either case, reflection, including eventual decision, is an essential part of the learning process.

From a teacher's point of view, reflection is the most essential part. As we have seen earlier, a teacher has virtually no control over a person's starting point. That is a given, the combined result of nature and cultural environment. In much the same way, the teacher has little control over a person's significant experiences; most of them occur in the student's day-to-day life *outside* the classroom. Even when we do attempt to provide such experiences, we have no guarantee that they in fact will be significant to the students. So the major role of the teacher becomes one of attempting to recognize significant experiences when they occur and then of facilitating the students' reflection on them. The teacher, then, is primarily a facilitator of reflection. For this reason, we will review now the tools the teacher has available in religious education for facilitating reflection. First, however, it will be helpful to expand a little on what we mean by reflection as an integral step in the learning process.

Reflection, as used here, is what we normally understand by our everyday use of the word: thinking, pondering, weighing alternatives, taking time to step back to take a good look at ourselves. As such it is a very personal act, a very interior act. It involves the dimension of solitude. On the other hand, reflection by its very nature also involves the dimension of dialogue. Even if a person is alone, his reflection is a dialogue with himself. In fact, the root meaning of the word is "to bend back upon oneself," to step outside oneself and then to look back. So reflection is very personal; no one can do it for you. At the same time, it is dialogic; it involves "two" people even when alone.

This latter dimension is what makes it possible for the teacher to facilitate reflection. In many instances, the teacher is the second person, playing the role of alter ego or even devil's advocate. In instances when the teacher personally is not involved, he can structure the situation so the one doing the reflecting is placed in dialogue with another person. This other person may be a guest speaker, another student, even an author through his writings, film, or play. In any case, the teacher, as a facilitator of reflection, must provide an opportunity for dialogue. What, then, are the tools whereby the teacher provides this opportunity, and how and when can he use them most effectively?

The primary method for facilitating reflection is personal counselling, that is, dialogue with the teacher. This, unfortunately, is also the most difficult to arrange, hence it is beyond the scope of most teachers, at least in a formal sense. It involves too much time, especially when a large number of students are involved. It sometimes demands professional skills that not every religion teacher possesses. However, there are several things a religion teacher can do to make maximum use of this method. First, he can attempt to project to students his personal concern for them. That is, students should be able to begin to see the religion teacher not so much as an expert imparting knowledge but as a more experienced friend involved in the same life problems they face, as a person they really could talk to if the need arose. Obviously, no teacher can fake such an attitude. Nor can he expect to be liked and trusted by all his students. Yet, the effective religion teacher attempts to establish a "counselling" relationship with as many students as he can.

Religion teachers in most instances are very much interested in and concerned about their students. That is probably one of the basic motivations for teaching religion. The problem is that too often religion teachers simply don't know how to go about establishing this kind of relationship. This happens both in a school setting and in CCD.

Some teachers fear that "being friendly" with students will lead to discipline problems or lack of respect. This is true if "being friendly" is misinterpreted to mean identifying so much with the students that you begin to think and to act like them. Students don't want adults to "act like kids." They want adults to understand why kids act the way they do. So "being friendly" means the teacher allows the students to be themselves and tries to understand what "being themselves" really means. "Being friendly" also means preserving between yourself and the student the distance that is there simply because you are an adult: the distance of more experience, of objectivity, of a mature self-control. This is what students look for in teachers, at least in teachers they would turn to for help. For teachers in the early grades, maintaining this distance is quite natural. In the upper grades and especially in high school, teachers find it harder to maintain that balance between "acting like the kids" and being aloof and out of touch with the students.

Sometimes, too, teachers fail to establish a counselling relationship with students because of their own fear of their emotions. They feel awkward and threatened in situations that call for a display of sincere affection, concern, or even anger. Letting others know how we feel makes us vulnerable. It gives them a certain power over us. For many teachers, it seems too risky to give students that kind of power over them, especially if students are adolescents. We are not asking teachers to indulge in that warped kind of "confessional" honesty that is in vogue in some group and sensitivity experiences. The classroom is not an encounter or sensitivity group. But it should involve personal encounter and true sensitivity between the teacher and students.

From all we have seen thus far, it seems evident that the training of religion teachers, either professional or amateur, should include some training in those personal skills necessary for establishing and maintaining a counselling relationship. This training might include an exposure to the theory of transactional analysis, which is useful for the teacher both in understanding himself and in effectively communicating with students. Certainly a familiarity with the work of a man like Carl Rogers is valuable, particularly his book *Freedom to Learn*. Properly supervised encounter or communications labs are another training possibility for teachers. Whatever is helpful in enabling teachers to make better use of counselling opportunities should be part of their teacher preparation.

It is one thing to establish a counselling relationship with students; it is another to be available for conversation. Here concrete techniques are questionable since each teacher's circumstance will be unique. But there are some rules of thumb: Be available as much as you can; be patient; don't be afraid to initiate. Being available may mean anything from inviting students to drop in at your home to getting rid of the unlisted convent telephone number. Being patient means you may have to wait all year before students begin to seek you out for advice or counsel. Being willing to initiate means a direct invitation to an individual to stop by for a talk. The invitation often is the very thing a student is waiting to hear; he is ready, but he would never make that kind of move on his own. With younger children, of course, the teacher normally will do much of the initiating.

In addition to counselling, group discussion is an excellent means of facilitating reflection. Its use, of course, is quite limited before the junior-high years. But from that point on it can be the most effective day-to-day means for facilitating reflection. "Peer dialogue" definitely appeals to adolescents. Note that we stress group discussion belongs in the third step of the learning process, reflection. This doesn't mean a good group discussion can't become a significant experience in its own right. But a teacher should not attempt to plan a class or program in which discussion is to be the significant experience. In planning to use discussion, it is presumed that the students already have had a significant experience or that the teacher first will provide one. With that in mind, what are some guidelines to insure effective discussion?

First, we must distinguish between informal discussion and structured discussion. Informal discussion is more or less spontaneous; it takes place without much prompting or instructing. For example, if the students just sponsored a party for a nursing home, all the teacher need do is to provide a meeting place and perhaps some pizza and soft drinks. When an experience is both significant and fresh, students normally will begin to discuss it without prompting or with some minimal initiation like "Well, how do you think it went?" or "What did you think of that place?" The key, of course, is that the experience is both significant *and* fresh. If the students scattered immediately after the experience and then gathered a week later, chances for a spontaneous, informal discussion are nil.

If the experience is not fresh, the teacher should turn to a more structured approach. The elements of structured discussion include, first of all, an experience of some significance shared in common. That can't be stressed too much. Second, the teacher will want to establish a very concrete and (hopefully) action-oriented goal for the discussion. This might be: "Today, I want you to decide together whether or not our party for the elderly was worthwhile and to decide if we should follow it up with some other activity." (Note that the goal stresses the word "decide"; it avoids the word, "discuss.") This kind of concrete goal gives real direction and purpose to the discussion. It requires that students recall and evaluate the experience, and it initiates some thinking about broader implications, such as a follow-up activity. On the other hand, to simply invite students with words like "I want you to discuss what we did last week" or "Let's discuss the party we gave last week" provides no direction or motivation. Compounded by the time lag, the discussion will be short-lived or drift about aimlessly.

Besides a significant experience to discuss and a concrete goal for the discussion, there are several other aspects to structuring an effective discussion. The teacher will want to set up a time limit, usually one that is "too short." If you think it should take the students thirty minutes to reach their goal, give them twenty. This approach does two things. It applies a certain healthy pressure to stay at the task, and it is a safety valve in case the discussion begins to fall flat. Better to have students ask for more time if they need it than to worry about what you are going to do with the extra fifteen minutes you had planned for discussion.

The teacher also will want to establish a work atmosphere. Students should be seated around tables with paper, pencils, and whatever other aids they might need. Informal discussion can take place while lounging in soft chairs or lying about on the floor because the motivation to discuss is high. Such lounging and casualness is destructive when involved in a structured discussion.

Another element of structured discussion is the role the teacher plays. In an informal discussion, the teacher will normally participate, contributing observations and comments along with the students. In structured discussion, the teacher should not participate. If there is a concrete goal, proper motivation, and a time limit, students will tend to pursue the discussion on their own. The teacher isn't needed to "keep it going" or to give it direction; he has done that by providing a meaningful goal and a time limit. He enters only at the end when he asks for the conclusions.

This conclusion is a crucial element, and it is best handled through a spokesman or secretary (appointed by the group) when there are about five minutes left to the discussion. The spokesman can present the summary for the group. This summary is especially effective—and necessary—when a teacher has divided a larger class into several smaller groups for discussion.

After the summary has been presented, the teacher can participate actively. He can ask for clarifications from the group, how they arrived at the conclusion. He is free to challenge the decision, question the validity of their reasons, give his own personal views on the matter. Precisely because students feel the support of a group and because the teacher did not influence the outcome of the discussion, students are much more open to the teacher's view on the matter. Thus, the teacher is in a good position either to reinforce the students' views or to facilitate further reflection on the matter by his challenges and personal views.

Structured discussion, then, involves establishing a concrete goal related to a significant experience, setting a time limit, providing a work atmosphere, soliciting a report or summary, and then giving personal views on the matter either to reinforce or to challenge the group's conclusions.

This method of discussion, because it follows upon a common significant experience of the group, insures greater participation by all members. Insofar as everyone has shared the experience, everyone has something to say about it. It helps eliminate a common complaint about group discussion: Some students don't participate. Of course, some students do not participate, at least not vocally. But discussion based on a common experience is still an effective means for helping them reflect. They are "in dialogue" even though silent because they are hearing opinions and attitudes that touch on something they themselves are concerned about. Remember, half of dialogue is listening. Concern over silent members in a discussion often is misdirected; hesitancy to verbalize doesn't necessarily mean failure to reflect. And reflection is the purpose for structuring a discussion.

A final warning about discussion. As a teaching tool, it is only effective if students first have had a significant experience. The experience may be a field trip, a multi-media "light show," a simulation game, a particularly moving or provocative speaker. But something must have "happened" to the students before we can expect them to discuss. In ninety five percent of those cases where the discussion technique has failed in religion programs, it is because there was no significant experience or because the teacher presumed an experience was significant when in fact it missed the students entirely. A teacher simply can't ignore the principles involved in the learning process and expect discussion to work.

Closely related to group discussion as a means of facilitating reflection is the whole process of value clarification. Since so much already is available on value clarification, I won't attempt to explain it here. However, I do want to stress that for value clarification strategies to work, they must be situated in their proper place in the learning process: as tools to facilitate reflection on significant experiences. Like group discussion, value-clarification strategies presuppose that students have had experiences that provoked in them a need to clarify certain values in their lives. This brings us back one step further, namely, to the starting point in the learning process. At each stage in his growth, a person is open to certain experiences and, consequently, to clarifying certain values. For example, fourth graders can be helped to clarify such values as honesty, fair play, respect for the property of others. Strategies that involve clarifying such values as peace, the dignity of the human person, the value to be placed on human sexuality—these more properly belong in programs for adolescents, whose starting point indicates a readiness to deal with such concerns and who normally have had sufficient experiences to begin to provoke reflection on such values.

So while value-clarification strategies deserve an important place in the religion teacher's arsenal of techniques, the teacher should choose them in keeping with the students' starting point. Also in using them, the teacher should keep in mind that they are intended to facilitate reflection on an experience. They are not the experience itself.

Next in the list of available means to facilitate reflection are several long-standing techniques that are still very useful: the lecture, the film, songs, story telling, poetry, books, and articles. We can list here even some of the traditionally more academic exercises like the written or oral report, the panel discussion, the term paper, the debate. All of these still have value if used properly. Each sets up a "dialogue" between students and persons more experienced than themselves—persons, we would presume, who reflect the faith-life and values the teacher is trying to foster. Each of these techniques also could be the source of a significant experience that provokes reflection. A teacher may choose a particularly moving film to provide a significant experience to his class and follow this by a discussion to facilitate reflection. On the other hand, a teacher may choose to show a particular film to further facilitate reflection on a concern in which the students already are involved. This same principle is true of speakers, books, readings, and the many other tools mentioned. In one instance, a speaker could be chosen precisely in an attempt to provide a significant experience In another instance, the same speaker might be more effective as a means to facilitate reflection on a significant experience. Whether they are used to provide a significant experience or to facilitate reflection, these tools will be effective only if the teacher knows why he is choosing a particular one and then carefully ascertains that it fits both his purpose and the capacity of his students.

One other means of facilitating reflection, special to the teacher of religion, is prayer—liturgical, para-liturgical, personal. A well-planned liturgy with an appropriate choice of readings, songs, and homily can be very effective in fostering reflection on an experience common to students. Such an approach, of course, should not be purely utilitarian; the sacredness and mystery of the liturgy must be preserved and emphasized. With para-liturgical programs we have more flexibility. They can include such things as a Scripture service, a nonsacramental penance service, an agapé supper. Personal prayer is an area that needs continued encouragement by religion teachers. Periods of silence within the lesson often can be planned. Opportunities for spontaneous prayer should be provided. The private reading of Scripture, once students are ready for it, should be assigned or at least encouraged.

Prayer in its various forms has obvious value as a means of facilitating reflection. It can put students in dialogue with the Word of God. It is a direct way to shed the light of the Gospel on the questions that students are pondering. But like other means of facilitating reflection, it is governed by the principle that the significant experience must occur before prayer becomes a means of reflection. The form of prayer opportunity provided also must be in keeping with the capacity of the students. If the teacher keeps those principles in mind, however, he will discover that he can incorporate prayer opportunities into his planning much more often—not as something added on "because it is a religion class," but as an integral part of the learning process.

There is one final concern that needs to be explored in terms of this step in the learning process. It is the whole question of the final result of reflection, the decision to alter one's lifestyle, to incorporate a new value or attitude, to change behavior patterns.

The outstanding hallmark of the student's decision must be freedom. He has no control over the events that break in on him or over those the teacher programs. His inner dynamism to grow develops at its own independent pace. Likewise, insofar as the teacher tends to structure opportunities for reflection, his growth to some degree is directed by outside forces. However, one thing can't be programmed: the student's "yes" or "no." The teacher can do everything right. Yet, after reflection, the student can still say, "I choose to continue in my former lifestyle. I simply don't agree that the Christian value or truth you've presented is good for me." If the student didn't maintain this inner control, then teaching would be mere manipulation.

Why a student says "no" even after an excellent teaching effort remains a mystery. Yet, it is a mystery that permeated the teaching of Jesus. The American bishops stated in their pastoral letter, *To Teach us Jesus Did,* that we should model our own teaching on the motives and the methods of Jesus himself. Yet, Jesus' personal teaching career could be judged a total failure. He only succeeded in reaching a small handful of people, and even they needed the event of the Resurrection to really confirm them in his message. If Jesus, our model for teaching, encountered failure, it seems reasonable to conclude that this failure was not in his teaching method but in the hearts of his listeners. They not only had the freedom to say "no," they also exercised that freedom. Insofar as religion teachers model themselves after Jesus, they can anticipate that even effective teaching will sometimes (often?) evoke a "no" from their students. Or, if not a "no," at least a "not yet."

Chapter Six:
assimilation

From the teacher's point of view, assimilation, the last step in the learning process, is the most simple. From the learner's point of view, it is often the most difficult. For the teacher, it involves providing opportunities, advice, and encouragement. For the student, it is the moment of truth when he must begin to live out the subject of his reflection.

This "living out" can be painful for one of two reasons. Inexperience can make it awkward and confusing, as in the case of a student with a newly-found conviction that he should be more outgoing and friendly, less self-centered and introverted. He's not sure just what all this means or how to go about it, so he can anticipate many moments of social embarrassment and awkwardness. Another source of pain can be the very nature of the conviction. He may have become convinced that he should give more time and effort in the service of the poor or elderly. This means less time for himself and his own pleasure—no easy task to be sure.

Thus, the teacher plays a crucial role in helping the student to assimilate the decision. The goal of assimilation, of course, is to turn theory into practice, an ideal into a reality, a notion into an integral part of one's lifestyle. As mentioned above, the teacher can assist in three ways.

First, he can provide opportunities for such practice, chances to try out this new lifestyle. He might structure an activity himself or direct the student to already existing opportunities. An example of the first would be to plan a project for assisting the poor as a follow-up to a lesson on the Christian ideal of justice. Or he can direct students to an organization like the Vincent de Paul Society. In either case, the teacher is helping the student overcome both his inexperience and his own hesitation.

Advice, the second element in facilitating assimilation, means simply that: telling students what they can expect, what tends to work or not work, typical failures they can anticipate, little tricks for achieving success in this new lifestyle they are adopting. Advice has become the one thing most adults hesitate to give to young people, especially teenagers. In one sense, this is a healthy overreaction to a time when almost all teaching took the form of "advice giving." We can afford to back off from that kind of teaching for a while. But giving advice still has an integral role in the learning process. Once a student is determined to integrate a particular value into his life, he is most open, even eager, for advice. A coach, for example, still can teach almost exclusively by "giving advice," which is another word for coaching. Why? Because the students already have decided that they want to learn the particular skill the coach is teaching. In the same way, once a person has become convinced that prayer should be an integral part of his lifestyle, he is open to the advice of anyone with more experience than he. So while giving advice does not play much of a role in the first steps in the learning process, it still can function in that final step, assimilation.

Encouragement and praise are the third kind of teacher assistance. Precisely because this is the difficult stage for the learner, he needs encouragement and in particular the encouragement called praise. The successful coach knows when to praise his team for a job well done. In much the same way, a good teacher knows when to praise students for a service project well done, a liturgy carefully prepared, a display of thoughtfulness that was unsolicited.

In general, then, the religion teacher, in this last stage of the learning process, must provide opportunities, advice, and encouragement. Of the three, the latter two can't very well be programmed. They must be spontaneous and fit the situation as it arises. Providing opportunities, however, is something the teacher should consider as he plans his lesson. Some of the following guidelines might help in such planning.

First, the opportunities we talked about should be planned primarily in terms of the overall goal of the lesson. If the goal is to foster greater appreciation for how the sacrament of Penance should influence the life of the Christian, opportunities for action should relate to that goal: penance services, opportunities for confession, prayer service related to the spirit of forgiveness, opportunities to "do penance."

Second, such opportunities generally should be practices the students eventually can undertake themselves without the direction of the teacher. For example, the teacher might be able to organize a successful clean-up campaign among his sixth graders as a follow-up to a lesson on respect for God's creation. It may not have as much transfer value, however, as encouraging students to be more careful about disposing of litter on the way home from school each day. In the same way, to have students provide a party for the elderly may not be as useful in terms of assimilation as would encouraging each of them to "adopt" one elderly person for whom they would do one kind deed each week. The latter can be carried out alone; the former requires much organization and the kind of initiative we can't rightly expect of students without outside assistance.

The third guideline is to remember that these activities are opportunities to *practice* the new awareness, conviction, or value. Assimilation is a lifelong process. It needs to be reviewed and reapplied as a person matures, encounters new experiences, expands his insights. The activity that the teacher provides is just an initial help, something to get the new way of behaving beyond the initial awkwardness or confusion.

The fourth guideline is that the activities be within the capacity and resources of the students. That is, they must be realistic. To ask too much too soon is only to discourage a budding conviction. We can ask a third grader to share his candy; to give it *all* away might be too much. We can ask a sophomore to participate in a half-hour prayer service; to expect him to participate in an all-night vigil would obviously be overdoing it.

Fifth, such activities should have immediate meaning in the lives of students. They should be considered "practice" only in terms of the long-range goals of a mature faith-life. For students, these activities should be quite serious right now. We can afford to smile, for example, at the small child's efforts at prayer, knowing what mature prayer implies. However, we can't afford to smile at the fact that the small child *is* praying and praying in a manner appropriate to his age. From our point of view, it may be called practice. From the child's point of view, it is very real. So we must be careful to provide activities that not only are within the students' reach but also have real value in their eyes. Collecting food for the poor at Thanksgiving is only a gesture in terms of combating the real sources of poverty. But for the seventh grader, it can be most significant and an ideal way to begin assimilating into his lifestyle concern for the poor.

A rather obvious guideline, though often overlooked, is that such assimilation activities should relate to students' present state of life. For example, many marriage courses for seniors in high school suggest all kinds of things they should do after they are married, an event usually several years into the future. The courses would be more effective if they suggested activities students could begin now—ways to make them better communicators, ways to form certain habits of self-discipline or personal hygiene, ways to show respect for the person they are dating—all activities they can do *now*. Often this mistake is made because the curriculum didn't take into account the starting point of the students. The whole topic is too advanced, so it must follow that the practical opportunities for assimilation are available only in the future. Perhaps the classic example of this mistake is early Confirmation. By nature this is a sacrament for mature persons who have arrived at or consciously aspire to a life of integrated faith. The ideals of the sacrament suggest actions of a very mature nature, things like a total life commitment to service. To teach the very young about Confirmation implies that opportunities for assimilation must be postponed for some time—rendering the whole effort virtually useless.

Another guideline to use in planning opportunities for assimilation is to look as much as possible for already existing opportunities. Just as in providing the significant experience we should first look for "what's happening," so in assimilation we should look for programs, organizations, activities already provided. This has the effect of further rooting the experience in life and of giving students a chance to continue the action after the class disbands. For example, identifying a place where meaningful liturgy occurs is more helpful than trying to provide continuously such liturgies yourself. Introducing students to an active chapter of the Legion of Mary is more helpful than continuously structuring those opportunities for prayer and service that can be found in the Legion. To discover that such ideals are practiced "outside the classroom" is as important to assimilation as providing the opportunity to practice them.

One final guideline: Teachers should remember that no activity can of itself guarantee that students will assimilate the ideal or conviction into their lifestyle. If the student was free in the reflection stage of the learning process, he remains just as free at the point of assimilation. For example, a student may decide to make prayer an integral part of his life. The teacher can provide opportunities for prayer, plus advice and encouragement about leading a life of prayer. But if the whole experience begins to demand too much, the student may return to his former, more superficial lifestyle. This is his free decision. The teacher's responsibility is to provide opportunities for the students to assimilate the ideals into their lifestyles. But that is all the teacher can do. Faith-life is a free response to opportunities freely offered. The teacher can provide the opportunities; he can't control the response.

On the positive side, however, the teacher should remember that many times students will make applications we don't anticipate. While the student may not accept the invitation to "adopt" an elderly person at the local nursing home, he may begin to show much more consideration for a grandparent living with him or an elderly neighbor he once enjoyed harassing. So while it is essential that the teacher plan to provide opportunities for the students to "practice" their newly found conviction, the students' response to that "practice" never will be an absolute gauge of successful teaching. Students maintain the power to resist good teaching; they also maintain the power to make their own application for living out the insights they discover.

To sum up, then, the teacher should provide opportunities for students to test out or practice the new ideal, insight, or conviction they obtained through the religious education program. Such opportunities should be in keeping with the goal of the particular lesson, be actions the students eventually could undertake on their own, and be within the capacity and resources of the student—his intelligence, available time, emotional maturity. The activity should have both meaning and immediacy. And, finally, teachers should remember that students maintain the power to reject the ideal behind the activity and to reject a particular activity in favor of another.

It might be good to make a few additional observations about the final step in the learning process. We've alluded already to the fact that assimilation is in some ways a lifelong process. The ideal of prayer may be implanted very early in a person's life; the form it takes will continue to evolve as the person matures. But the ideal may lie dormant for a long time before it blossoms in action and ultimate assimilation. Let's not be too anxious, then, to equate successful religious education with performance. On the other hand, performance is the only legitimate way of evaluating what is effective. A paradox of sorts, to be sure, but one intended to keep us hopeful, humble, and professional as we attempt to share our own faith with the next generation.

Along the same lines, the assimilation of a value or insight into one's lifestyle may be relatively instantaneous. For example, each of the Apostles experienced a rather dramatic call. The very intensity of the experience precipitated reflection and consequent decision. Assimilation was simply (?) the following of Jesus, meeting his demands, learning to anticipate his expectations. Awkwardness, confusion, even doubt were all part of the process, but the fact is that none of them—except Judas—ever really turned back from their initial commitment. For the Apostles, Jesus became part of themselves and their destiny from the first moment they met him. There was still doubt and hesitation, but that is generally characteristic of assimilation.

Assimilation is probably where all real learning takes place, at least in the sense that "we learn by doing." In a single sentence, assimilation is implementing a decision based on reflection that was prompted by a significant experience. As teachers of religion, we must provide opportunities for students to try out the ideals we fostered in the first steps of the learning process. We must provide practical advice about what they do and encouragement and praise as they do it.

Chapter Seven:
lesson planning

Having examined each of the steps in the learning process, we are now in a position to attempt a synthesis. One way to do this is by reviewing the principles governing lesson planning.

We begin by making a distinction between a *lesson* plan and a *session* plan. A lesson plan embraces the full scope of the learning process. It has a goal that is based on knowledge of the students' starting point. It provides a significant experience, activities to facilitate reflection, and opportunities for assimilation. As such, a lesson plan can be defined as all those activities designed by the teacher to reach a particular learning goal. A *session* plan, on the other hand, is simply a segment of a lesson plan; it has a sub-goal related to the overall goal of the lesson. For example, a lesson plan may call for one session to provide a significant experience, several more to facilitate reflection, and an additional session to facilitate assimilation.

A lesson plan, therefore, provides an overview that dictates what is to be accomplished in each session. As such, it implies no fixed amount of time; its length is determined by the goal of the lesson. A session, on the other hand, usually is defined as a prescribed period, say fifty minutes, often determined by circumstances, established schedules, convenience. For example, a lesson plan could call for six fifty-minute sessions, or it could call for a full weekend of intensive activity, whichever seems indicated for achieving the goal.

This distinction between lesson plan and session plan is important to religious education. Too often we think only in terms of sessions, not lessons. The curriculum suggests that we cover twenty topics. We have forty sessions available to us. Our answer: two sessions on each topic. That is session planning. Unfortunately, it ignores the learning process. Not all topics may be of equal value; some will require more time to learn than others. Session planning insures only that we will cover the material, not that any learning is going to take place.

Given the same twenty topics and the same forty available sessions, we would operate much differently using the lesson-plan approach. For example, there would be no attempt to think in terms of twenty goals for the year. Rather, four or five would be identified as suggested by the students' starting point. Then a plan would be developed to reach each of these goals, using as many sessions for each goal as the nature of the goal warrants. One goal may be reached in four sessions, another could take ten, a third goal might require three sessions at the beginning of the year followed by two more at the very end of the year—all as part of the same lesson plan. What happens to the twenty topics? They would be dealt with in relation to the goals. One topic might be covered in the process of providing a significant experience. Others could be introduced in the process of reflection. Others may be viewed in terms of possible opportunities for assimilation.

The characteristics, then, of this comprehensive lesson planning are that it is built around goals, not topics, and it embraces all phases of the learning process sequentially rather than in terms of a fixed number of unrelated sessions.

Several steps are involved in this kind of lesson planning:

1. After deciding on a general goal in keeping with the students' starting point, clarify for yourself what is meant by the goal.

2. Next define the goal of the lesson in terms of:
   (a.) The concrete behavior you hope to evoke, making any adaptions called for by the cultural environment.
   (b.) The intellectual (theological) rationale supporting such behavior.

3. In light of this concrete goal, determine the best way to provide a significant experience.

4. Next, identify the various ways you can facilitate reflection on the experience and the kinds of intellectual imput you want to introduce into the process.

5. Finally, determine the kinds of assimilation opportunities you will want to provide.

The first step in lesson planning is a rather personal one, but very important. Basically, it entails putting yourself into the subject matter. For example, if you are to teach prayer during the course of the year, you don't begin by asking *how* you are going to teach. Rather, you begin by asking *what* you are going to teach. What does prayer mean to you? How would you define it? How large a part does it actually play in your life? When did you first learn the value of prayer? How did you learn it? These kinds of questions illustrate what we mean by clarifying the goal for yourself. The more clearly you understand what is meant by the goal, the more you will be able to sincerely witness to it and to facilitate reflection and assimilation. If the topic isn't "real" for you, if you aren't that sure of it or that excited about it, you probably cannot be of much help to students.

So the process of clarifying the subject for yourself is a very important part of teaching in general and lesson planning in particular. Such clarification might involve some additional homework on your part: background reading, looking up a few definitions, filling the gaps in your own experience. In any event, before any actual lesson planning and teaching, the religion teacher will want to decide what the topic means to him and how well he understands it.

The next step is to translate your own insights into a concrete goal for your students. (We are assuming that the general topic or goal is in keeping with students' starting point.) To translate this into a working goal for students requires three elements. First, the goal must be expressed in terms of the specific behavior desired, a behavior that takes into account the cultural environment of the students. For example, though the general goal, prayer, might be the same for both an inner-city group and a suburban group, the specific behavioral goal for each group might be quite different. The goal for the inner-city group might be that they begin to feel comfortable, as a group, with spontaneous prayer. The suburban students might have already reached that point, so the goal would go beyond it to another dimension or form of prayer. In any event, the goal always should be as concrete and as specific as possible. It can mention names, times, places, very specific actions. An unsuitable goal for fifth graders, in terms of specifics, might read: that the students learn to respect law. A better goal would read: that the fifth graders become more observant of the school rules regarding littering and also show greater respect to Mrs. Smith, the crossing guard.

A concrete and culturally-adapted behavioral goal still needs a statement of the reasoning, rationale, and theology behind the behavior. Obeying school rules and respecting crossing guards are good, of course. But unless students have some insight into why they are good, the process begins to smack of conditioning, not learning. This second part of the goal should summarize the kind of insight you hope to provide and the faith or theology implications behind the behavior. In terms of traditional teaching, this part of the goal is an expression of the "content" you hope to teach. Thus, the second part of the behavioral goal just mentioned might read: "because the students understand the positive value of obeying laws in general and the Ten Commandments in particular." Such a goal gives you definite direction; you will want to facilitate reflection on the value of law, and particularly the value of the Ten Commandments. It also sets limits. You are not trying to exhaust the theology related to the Ten Commandments at this stage in the students' growth. You are just trying to introduce them to the fact that these Commandments exist, come from God, and are very helpful as guides for our lives.

Of all the steps in lesson planning, stating your goal in this twofold way is the most important. Everything else you decide will be determined largely by how you define your goal. The more concrete, precise, and clear it is, the easier you will be able to determine the best means for achieving it. Vague goals evoke vague planning. Goals that are too comprehensive don't give adequate direction. A carefully defined goal is about eighty percent of a good lesson plan.

Once you have formulated such a goal, you are ready to determine the next element in the lesson plan, the significant experience. In the example goal above, you are given some definite clues as to what kind of experience you need. It should involve school rules, littering, traffic laws. If, for example, a child recently had been injured at a school crossing, that experience itself might be sufficient for the class to reflect on the value of certain laws. If the principal recently has kept everyone after school to clean up unwarranted litter, that might serve as your experience. You obviously can't foresee such events, but you should incorporate them into your plan whenever they fit your goal.

In the absence of such gratuitous significant experiences, your planning should range over all the other means you have for providing a significant experience—field trip, work project, simulation related to law and order, etc. In any case, your lesson plan must include an activity you have chosen to provide a significant experience.

The nature of the significant experience often will determine your choice of activities for reflection, the next step in the lesson plan. If a small child had been hurt at a school crossing, for example, students (fifth graders in our example) could be asked to make safety posters to display around the school or in the windows of local stores. This kind of reflection is very well suited to the age group, and it provides ample opportunity for the teacher to begin to give some of the input suggested by the intellectual dimension of the goal. The one thing to keep in mind in planning the reflection is that you must anticipate how and when you hope to bridge from the particular significant experience to the broader implications contained in the goal. You must ask yourself how and when you are going to make a transition, for example, from considering traffic laws to considering God's law. For this reason, a lesson plan may have to include several sessions for reflection and several different activities to facilitate reflection. With high-school students, the transition from a particular experience to possible broad implications usually can be initiated by asking some well-timed questions—the students are intellectually capable of seeing such relationships on their own. With younger students, the teacher often will have to help students see the connection between a particular event and a general principle. So teacher input must be planned accordingly.

Whereas deciding on a proper statement of the goal is the most critical aspect of the lesson plan, planning the various means to facilitate reflection is the most technical. It often will require the most attention. Remember, the best definition of a teacher is a person who facilitates reflection.

The last step in this lesson-planning process is to determine opportunities for the students to assimilate this new insight—say the positive value of law—into their daily life. If the goal has been defined properly, it usually will indicate some concrete actions you might want to initiate. In the sample goal, specific mention was made of littering and respect for the crossing guard. So the teacher might suggest the class undertake an anti litter campaign in the school. Or he might suggest the class prepare and deliver thank-you notes to the crossing guard. It should be noted that often the assimilation activities will take place outside the classroom. The lesson plan may not call for a session devoted to assimilation but simply require that the teacher initiate a certain project or activity for the students to undertake when outside class. Some classroom follow-up may be planned, however, like asking for reports, giving advice, praising success, holding a prayer service to celebrate what has been done. In any event, the good lesson does call for definite plans for providing assimilation activities.

Each of the above steps should include a decision regarding length of time needed, the place(s) for the activity, particular dates, and the like. Thus a completed lesson plan becomes a kind of master schedule covering several days (in a school setting) or several weeks (in a CCD program). If this kind of planning seems long and involved, keep in mind you aren't planning for one session. You are planning a method of reaching a particular goal that could involve as many as ten sessions. You might need only four or five such plans to cover an entire teaching year.

This kind of planning insures more effective teaching since it respects the principles of learning process we have been examining. It also intends to eliminate that sense of panic and urgency many teachers experience when they are faced each week with the question "What am I going to do for the next class?" The lesson plan indicates what you will want to do and why. All that's left is some immediate preparation and attention to details not included in the plan. The whole experience of teaching becomes more purposeful, calm, intentional. A teacher will have the feeling he is getting somewhere insofar as his lesson plan unfolds the way he anticipated.

This kind of lesson planning also facilitates evaluation; now each session has a certain aspect of the learning process that it should fulfill. For example, if a planned significant experience was not successful, you will know it. Rather than go on to the next planned session, you can attempt first to provide another experience. Or if a particular method of reflection has turned the students off and you feel that they have not achieved the kind of insight you had hoped, you can try again before going on to the next step. Evaluation isn't something that takes place at the end of each session. If a session failed, it needs to be repeated in a new format. If it was successful, you can go with confidence to the next activity.

Some teachers may ask what the difference is between this approach to lesson planning and the unit concept used in most curriculum planning and textbook formats. There is a very important difference. A lesson plan embraces all the steps in the learning process and provides all the activities necessary to reach a particular behavioral/intellectual goal. A unit is typically a series of logically related topics to be covered. While a unit does not necessarily ignore the principles of the learning process, it is not structured around them. Most often the goal of a unit is to impart a body of knowledge in a logical fashion. A lesson plan, on the other hand, is psychologically designed around a goal that is behavioral as well as intellectual. Because the goal of religious education is to effect a change in lifestyle and to foster a personal relationship with God, rather than simply to impart certain knowledge about God, the unit approach, at least as defined above, is not well suited. It may result in knowledge but not necessarily in learning.

Our in-depth analysis of the learning process and its applicability to comprehensive lesson planning underscores two premises raised in the beginning of this book: 1—that religious educators already have at their disposal the necessary resources for successful teaching, and 2—that these resources can be used more effectively than they have been in the past.

Chapter Eight:
parent, parish, teacher

Until now, we have been concerned with how knowledge of the learning process can assist the religion teacher in his task, either in the school or in the CCD setting. But what implications might this same learning process have for the role of parents in the religious education of their children? What can it tell us about the role of the parish? And how are these roles of teacher, parent, and parish interrelated?

Official documents of the Church consistently have maintained that parents are the primary educators of their children. The recent pastoral letter, *To Teach as Jesus Did,* reaffirms this role. An understanding of the learning process takes us one step further. It clarifies *why* parents are the primary teachers, and it specifically indicates *how* they can (and do) fulfill this role.

No one is in a better position to understand a child's starting point than his parents. Teachers often have to depend on the general principles of psychological development to know what a child may be ready to learn; they don't have sufficient contact to know fully each individual child. Parents, however, tend to know this almost instinctively. Constant contact, motivated by love and concern, gives them an ongoing sensitivity to and awareness of each child. Personality traits, strengths and weaknesses of character, aptitudes, talent and interests—all these are known to parents. More importantly, subtle changes in personality, interest, and capacities also are noted continuously. This doesn't mean parents are omniscient. Even the most sincere and best educated parents sometimes will misread a child and will make a mistake in terms of readiness to learn. They may "push" music lessons too soon, expect better grades than are realistic, assume the child is ready for a personal responsibility that he is not yet equipped to handle. In general, though, parents are still in the best position to know the starting point of their child. This is true not just in terms of when it's best to learn to ride a two-wheeler or when the child is old enough to go to summer camp. It is also true of religious education. First Communion and first confession are two areas where more parents have assumed the primary responsibility for preparing the child and for deciding when the child is ready. However, parental knowledge of their children virtually extends to every stage of the child's readiness for the particular aspects of religious education.

Ideally, then, parents should set the goals for each year of their child's religious education. At least parents are in the better position to analyze critically the proposed goals of a program or textbook for their children. Yet, one unfortunate fact clouds this ideal and limits parents' capacity to assume this role. Too often their ideas reflect a time when religious education was viewed basically as imparting knowledge of the faith. Consequently, many parents think of goals more in terms of facts to be imparted than in terms of behavior to be cultivated or a faith *relationship* to be fostered. This produces a kind of blind spot among too many parents. They want their children to "learn" ideas that the youngsters are not ready for and that often have no connection with their present life experiences.

Dialogue between the professional catechist and parents seems the best way out of this dilemma. On the one hand, professionals must listen very carefully to what parents tell them. Too often catechists ignore a parent's complaints and suggestions. They forget that parents, even with the limitation just pointed out, are still in a better position to know what their own children are ready to learn. Yet it is also the task of professionals to attempt to free parents from certain misconceptions about the nature of religious education. When a religion program is built upon such dialogue, there is a much greater chance that the proposed goals will be realistic. Just as important, these goals will be endorsed by the parents, something that still is lacking in many religious education programs.

If parents are in the better position to know the starting point of their children, they are in an equally good position to be aware of the significant experiences taking place in their children's lives. Some time ago an entire family, including several young children, died from asphyxiation while spending a weekend in a rented cottage. The mother of two girls, who were friends and playmates of the dead children, talked with her daughters about death, about what a Christian believes, about her own feelings in the face of this tragedy. This is something any alert mother would do, realizing how deeply her children were disturbed by the experience.

Such instances can be multiplied a thousandfold in every family. Parents always will be in a good position to recognize the significant experiences in their children's lives. The broken heart of a sixteen-year-old girl, the excitement of "making the team," the tragedy of a lost pet, the wonder involved in seeing Grand Canyon on a family trip—these are simple examples of the kinds of experiences that fill the everyday life of a family. Any one of them is potentially significant for the growing child, and most are unknown to the teacher. Yet these are some of the best moments for learning what faith-life is all about. As teachers, we hope for such experiences; we attempt to create them when they are lacking. Parents, however, observe them constantly.

We said earlier that the teacher himself can be a significant experience to his students because of his personal witness. How much more true that is of parents. For the first several years of a child's life, parents are virtually his only really significant experience. Everything that happens to the child is somehow related to and filtered through the ongoing experience of his parents' love. Even as the child grows older, his parents normally remain the *most* significant of the various experiences he has. The example (witness) of parents always will be more important to the child's religious education than anything that happens in a formal religion program. This is rightfully frightening to any parent. How often, for example, has a parent "seen himself" in the small child playing house. Actions, subtle gestures, exact quotes from us are used as the child fantasizes about going shopping, cooking supper, reading the newspaper. Much of this is charming, of course, but then we hear or see something not so pleasant. A vulgar expression, a sharp tone of voice, a selfish gesture—these too are mimicked by the child. All this illustrates the pervasive influence the parent has on the child's formation, a formation that extends ultimately to the foundations for his future faith-life.

Much the same can be said for the parent's role in facilitating reflection. Precisely because the parent usually is the first to be aware of significant experiences and often is involved in those experiences first-hand, he is in the best circumstance to facilitate the child's reflection on the experience. The parent is also in the better relationship for such reflection. We said earlier that the best form of facilitating reflection is personal counsel—the old-fashioned heart-to-heart talk. When the child is young, parents are naturally the ones he will turn to for such a talk. This same relationship, with certain modification, can be maintained throughout adolescence.

The example of the mother discussing death with her two daughters is typical of the kind of talk that helps children think through and evaluate the real meaning of their experience. Unfortunately, many parents begin to feel uncomfortable with such topics, especially if they lead to points of "theology." Just as often, adults can feel uneasy about conversation that requires them to reveal some of their own deep feelings, fears, doubts, and convictions about their faith. Somehow many of us have grown up with the idea that these things are too private. Even between husband and wife such conversation is sometimes avoided.

Nonetheless, parents are still in the better position to facilitate reflection on many aspects of the child's growing faith-life. Since we have defined the teacher's essential task in the learning process as that of facilitating reflection, we have one more reason for reaffirming that parents are and should be the primary teachers for their children. For that reason, helping parents gain confidence and skill in communicating with their children is a most important task for the professional religion teacher. This is especially true for parents of teenagers.

Finally, parents have a key role to play in the process of assimilation. Opportunities to live out new insights are built into the family structure. As the child grows in his awareness of the value of prayer, the family's prayer life becomes an opportunity for him. As he becomes aware of his responsibility to share, his relationships with his brothers and sisters are ready opportunities for assimilation. Nothing artificial needs to be provided in the normally functioning family. Parents, insofar as they are attempting to guide and to structure their family's life according to their own faith convictions, automatically will be providing an environment for the child to assimilate each new faith insight into his lifestyle

If a special activity should be needed to assist assimilation, parents, usually the first to know, are in a position to initiate such an activity. It is a common experience today, for example, that teenagers begin to rebel against Sunday Mass attendance. For various reasons, they regard it as meaningless, even hypocritical. A wise parent, recognizing this experience, can help the child reflect on his reasons for not wanting to go, isolating sound reasons from imagined ones. In the process, the child usually realizes that he is rejecting not so much the idea of Mass but how it is celebrated in his parish church. The parent then can suggest attending Mass at different parishes for a while until the child finds one that better suits his needs. A teacher in the same case would not have the authority to suggest this rather unorthodox solution without risking a reprimand from the pastor or the wrath of parents who could misunderstand the teacher's intentions.

It appears that parents, at least theoretically, are in a better position than anyone else to teach religion to their children. Does this mean we should leave the task of teaching religion exclusively to parents, shut down our schools, and disband our CCD programs? Not quite. But it may mean some important restructuring of both as instruments for teaching religion. We will consider these implications in the next chapter. Now, however, let us take a closer look at the role of the religion teacher in light of the primary role of parents just described.

We must distinguish between the professional teacher and the volunteer. The professional religion teacher is a person who has received formal education in theology, psychology, and methodology, and consequently makes his living, at least in part, by teaching religion. How much formal education in these fields constitutes a person as a professional? It should be at least the same amount of training that is necessary to constitute a person as a professional teacher in any other field.

A volunteer would be any person who does not define himself as a professional teacher. While equipped with strong personal convictions about his religion and some general background and knowledge, he recognizes a need for some ongoing assistance by a professional teacher if he is to function effectively.

The professional teacher's role will be quite different in many respects from the volunteer. His task basically is to use his professional training to assist parents and volunteer teachers in their roles. As such he is a resource person. By talking with parents, he helps them arrive at realistic goals for the religious education of their children at each stage. He does this by helping parents understand more fully the multifaceted nature of growth in faith-life, by freeing them from the too narrow concept of religion as facts. The professional also has a responsibility to enrich parents' understanding of the stages of psychological development, usually through adult education programs dealing with child and adolescent psychology. This too should be a shared experience; parents have much practical knowledge that will qualify the theoretical treatment of psychological development.

The professional teacher's role in providing significant experiences is primarily to supplement what already is taking place in the students' life and to provide those specialized experiences that parents cannot normally offer. These include a weekend COR program for high school students, a special penance service for fourth graders, a special speaker known for his ability to reach freshmen, and so forth. These specialized experiences must be looked at realistically. They are supplemental to life, and usually they will be aimed at stimulating reflection on a very specific aspect of faith-life. As such, they can be planned ahead and organized into a regular curriculum. The number of meetings scheduled for students, given the supplemental or specialized purpose of these meetings, can in many instances be reduced, thus increasing the potential effectiveness of each experience. Decreasing the number of formal sessions, however, would assume that parents have been prepared to handle the day-to-day "teaching."

In facilitating reflection, the professional teacher's role is twofold. On the one hand, he is responsible for providing parents with ongoing education in theology and communication skills so that they can become more confident in their task of explaining aspects of the faith to their children. This means the professional teacher either is involved directly in adult education or must insure that others are providing it to the parents. The professional teacher also is responsible for facilitating reflection on those special experiences he provides students. It is the professional teacher's responsibility to work more directly with older students who are ready for reflection on more complex or sophisticated elements of theology. Since this kind of reflection is often done best within a formal peer setting, such as a discussion, attending a lecture, viewing a film, and the like, parents would be hard pressed to provide such opportunities. Nor should they be expected to deal with some of the more complex questions in the same way as the professional teacher. In fact, the professional teacher's role in facilitating reflection increases around the time of junior high school, as parental influence diminishes and peer influence takes over.

In terms of formal programs of religious education, an important implication emerges from this emphasis on working with older students. If we must drop any part of a program, it would seem more logical to drop the earlier grades since parents are in a much better position to facilitate all steps of the learning process for the younger child. While they continue to maintain a primary role in teaching the child even as he enters adolescence, parents naturally will find it more difficult to provide experiences and to facilitate reflection on certain important areas of faith-life. Hence, they will need the assistance of the professional teacher much more during this period.

In the area of assimilation, much the same thing can be said about the teacher's relationship to parents. Certain opportunities for assimilation require formal structures, peer groups, activities apart from the family: participating in a peer liturgy or a group service project, experiencing a communal penance service. Even the young child has a need for opportunities that an individual family is not equipped to provide. Thus there is the need for some formal program of assimilation opportunities, in keeping with the particular goal of the religion program at the time.

Though the parent is and always will be the primary teacher of religion to his children, he also needs and has a right to demand some professional assistance all along the way. The relationship between parent and professional teacher, then, is ideally one of mutual cooperation. The professional teacher is in the service of parents, assisting them. The parent must do his part, however, if the service provided by the professional teacher is to be effective. Quite literally, parent and professional teacher need each other.

What about the volunteer? His role and importance are in no way diminished because he is not a professional. Though he depends directly on the assistance of the professional catechist, he is also an extension of the professional teacher. While not required to provide adult education to parents—he usually will be on the receiving end of such education—he will assist the professional in providing structured experiences, facilitating reflection, and initiating activities for assimilation. As such, he also is serving parents, assisting them in their task. In many instances, parents will need the help of such volunteers much the same as they need the professional. Volunteers, on the other hand, must regard themselves as assisting parental teaching, not replacing it.

These distinctions should help define more realistically what can be expected of volunteers and what volunteers can expect of themselves. Volunteers have a right to demand professional leadership and assistance in their task. They should not feel they have the full responsibility for the children's religious education. Parents should recognize the specialized role of the volunteer: as an extension of the professional teacher, but not possessing the same degree of knowledge; as supplemental to parental teaching responsibility, but not a replacement for it.

Having explored the related functions of parents and teachers, we turn now to the role of the parish. The term "parish" can have two meanings. It can refer to the administrative team in the parish: pastor, associates, council, board of education, and the like. It also can mean the entire faith community, as when the parish gathers for liturgy, or when the parish donates food and clothes to assist earthquake victims.

Parish viewed as administration has a very critical task in religious education. It must provide whatever professional assistance parents will need to fulfill their task of fostering the faith in their children. This professional assistance may take the form of policy decisions regarding the maintenance of a parochial school, hiring professional catechists, the job descriptions of the pastor and his associate. It also would include ongoing adult education in theology, psychology, communication skills, etc., and a certain amount of structured programming for children and youth. In short, from an administrative point of view a parish has a serious obligation to establish policies and to provide funds adequate to insure that parents receive continous *professional assistance* in their task of teaching their children. "Professional" means fully qualified catechists to work both with parents and children. "Assistance" means the parental role remains (becomes?) central. Even a parochial school, no matter how excellent, can be regarded only as supplementary and assisting. Too often both parent and parish have viewed the parochial school as supplanting the parents' role.

The parish viewed as a faith community also has an essential role in the whole process of religious education. It provides the environment in which the efforts of both parent and professional teacher can prosper. The parish must be an example of what is meant by particular aspects of faith-life. If concern for the poor is under consideration, parent or professional teacher should be able to point to the action of the faith community in that regard. They should be able to direct the child or youth to participation in parish's work in this area. In the same way, when mutual respect, meaningful worship, or a strong sacramental life is at issue, the parent and teacher should be able to direct the students' attention to the life and activity of the parish as a living example.

If there is any hope for successful religious education, either in the home or in the structured program, the parish must emphasize its role as faith community. As stated in the *General Catechetical Directory* (#35): "Catechesis, finally, demands the witness of faith both from the catechists and from the ecclesial community (parish), a witness that is joined to an authentic example of Christian life and to a readiness for sacrifice. . . . If such witness is lacking, there arises in the listeners an obstacle to the acceptance of God's word." If we were to look for one single element that has caused much of our failure in religious education, I personally think it is lack of this effective witness on the part of most parishes. Often their very size and consequent impersonalism make it impossible for them to be an example of a faith community. Often, too, we must admit, unfortunately, that the level of authentic Christian faith present among adults is simply not sufficient to inspire children and youth to pursue a life of faith in their own right, despite the best efforts of individual parents and dedicated professional and volunteer teachers.

If parent, teacher, and parish are all involved together in handing on the faith to the next generation, all three must cooperate, and each must fulfill its own role. Insofar as the parish is failing to provide this essential environment and witness, the seeds of faith planted by parents and teachers have little chance to mature and bear fruit in their own time. Are we failing as parents or teachers? Or are we failing as parish? We must each make that judgment for ourselves.

Chapter Nine:
implications for the future

A proper understanding of the learning process has value beyond the present needs of religion teachers. It provides insights into two major trends that are central to the future development of religious education: family-centered catechetics and greater emphasis on the faith community. The learning process also sets guidelines for determining the role and structure of religious education in the coming years.

The single most common trend in catechetical circles today is the movement toward family catechetics or family-centered catechetics. This movement is not just one more in a long string of innovations. It is a logical maturing of the whole development of religious education in the past fifty years.

Granted, educators have returned to this model (it was popular in the late forties and fifties in avant-garde groups like Grailville) partially for negative reasons. Schools have declined; CCD programs often have proved ineffective. An economical and pastorally sound alternative needs to be found. It is no accident, however, that of all the possible alternatives, the family-centered model has begun to emerge as the dominant trend. Logically, psychologically, sociologically, and theologically, it is the most valid of all catechetical models. This trend is also quite timely as a renewal of the family unit itself, now quite literally an endangered species.

The learning process, which both justifies and dictates the primary role of parents in religious education, will be most helpful to pastors and catechists in the difficult task of shifting from our present models to the family model. The process explains the reasoning behind al the documents concerning the rights and responsibilities of parents. Further, it helps clarify the relationship between the parent, the professional catechist, and the parish.

If the learning process gives support to the movement toward family-centered programs, it gives equal emphasis to a second dominant concern in contemporary religious education, the faith community. The family needs the faith community's witness, support, and professional assistance if the religious education of children is to be effective. The community is the forum in which faith is experienced and lived out by the individual family. Active, responsible membership in that community is the goal of the parents' efforts to educate their children.

On the practical side, a proper understanding of the faith community's role in the learning process has begun to demand that the very structure of the local parish be reevaluated. The large parish with no clear sociological, cultural, or economical identity is simply untenable. One reason is it makes an effective program of religious education impossible. This is a serious statement, but it flows logically from an analysis of the nature of Church, of faith, and of religious education.

The greatest task of religious educators today is not curriculum development, methodology, or sound theology. It is the developing of alternative models to our traditional parochial structure. These models must insure the degree of personal interaction between the members, both adult and children, necessary for effective witness, worship, and support (significant experiences of lived faith). Until such models are developed, piloted, and implemented, all other work in religious education will continue to be impeded seriously if not rendered totally ineffective.

While the restructuring of parishes is imperative for effective religious education, it is usually beyond the scope of the religious educator to accomplish. This kind of restructuring normally lies in the hands of the bishop, or at least the pastor. Whoever does the restructuring, he will run into very practical obstacles. For example, the financial base for the Church, if we are realistic, is the parish with its carefully determined boundaries, its tithes, and its diocesan assessment. Add to this the tradition implied in present parish structures. Also add the fact that breaking parishes into smaller units usually requires the ministry of additional priests, and their numbers are decreasing rather than increasing. Nor can we forget the mobility of present society. So even if religion educators had the authority, they still would find it difficult to impose new models to replace present parish structures.

Despite these obstacles, the challenge remains. Parents, as the primary educators, will shirk their duty or find themselves inadequate unless they can be members of a vital faith community. Hence, religious education, for both the immediate present and well into the future, must be concerned essentially with family catechesis and faith community (parish structure).

What about the school and the CCD program if family and parish is the primary concern of religious educators? A little historical perspective may be helpful in understanding the potential role of these two models in the future of religious education. Parochial schools, as we have experienced them in the United States, were born out of genuine faith communities—people with strong social, ethnic, economic, or geographical ties and ultimately welded together by their common faith and a common Catholic tradition. In these communities, the children grew in faith within the family; faith was an integral part of all their parents said and did. Parents, in turn, were supported by the faith community at large, which reinforced the values and convictions that the children experienced at home.

This was a real community, a visible community in which a youth could aspire to assume an active role as he matured. In this parish, a school was established to protect children against hostile theologies and values prevalent in the public school. Its purpose, though not formulated in these terms, simply was to facilitate reflection and to give logical (apologetic) explanations for the faith the children experienced every day within the family and the larger faith community. (Of course, the academic education was desired to insure that the children would have sufficient skills to better themselves economically.)

Rooted as they were in faith communities, the schools worked magnificently. No one can argue that the growth and success of the Church in America, and of many individual Catholics within the Church, can be attributed in large part to the parochial school system. What is too often ignored is that the success of the school system depended on an even deeper base. That base was the local parish, a true faith community. What we are witnessing today is not so much the demise of the Catholic school system as a demise of faith communities that made the support of such a school system possible.

Within this same historical perspective, we can better appreciate the development of the Confraternity of Christian Doctrine. It took its origins from the school experience and the school model. When CCD was conceived, no one doubted the value of the parochial school. The only problem was that not all parishes could support such schools or find sufficient religious to staff them. CCD was intended as a viable alternative in *those* situations, not as an improvement on religious education as such. Conceived as a stepchild, it remains one to this day. But wherever CCD programs were established within a vital faith community, they worked for the same reason the school worked. The real education was taking place within the family and within the parish community as a whole. CCD added a necessary refinement to this education.

If CCD programs are failing today, it is for the same reason the schools are dying: a disappearing faith community. But rather than unite to solve this common problem of parishes that are no longer faith communities, the school and the CCD are competing with each other. Even worse, they often are the two poles around which a parish divides itself, thus condemning both school and CCD to ineffectiveness.

Let us assume, as is the case in some places already, that a parish is a faith community of the type that gave birth to the parochial school and its alternative, the CCD program. In this situation, what is the role of the school and CCD? Both are valid models for religious education. Both have essentially the same task: to facilitate orderly reflection on the significant experiences provided in family and parish, to give more factual and logical development to the meaning of those experiences than can be provided conveniently within the family, and to offer certain peer group experiences of faith.

Given these similarities, each has certain advantages that the other lacks. The school, because it has more continuous contact with students, normally can do a more thorough job of providing factual and logical development of the faith as it is experienced. However, a fifty-minute period within the confines of a classroom doesn't lend itself to a long-range project like a field trip, an overnight, a guest speaker, or informal discussion.

CCD programs, because they are (should be) more flexible, can program these types of experiences and facilitate reflection in ways the schools find difficult if not impossible. At the same time, because its access to students is limited, the CCD program has been forced to confine itself to activities and more "dramatic" events simply to hold the students in attendance, thus making it difficult to deal with content in any serious or in-depth manner.

It is not surprising that each goes to excess in what it is best equipped to do. For example, the school tends to overteach, to hold too many classes, to over-intellectualize, to reduce faith to facts to be remembered rather than a relationship to be lived. CCD programs, on the other hand, have been caricatured by parents and students alike as "fun and games," superficial programs that never lead to serious questioning or systematic study.

The concern is not whether the school or the CCD program is a valid model with a genuine role to play in religious education. The question is whether both can learn from each other and cooperate with each other to the degree necessary for their mutual survival. (The survival of the school as an *academic* alternative to the public school's *academic* program is an entirely different matter, which, though very important, is beyond the scope and purpose of this book.)

With this historical perspective, we now can raise the question: What will be the structure and function of the parochial school and CCD program of the future? Both will be rooted in authentic parishes, in viable faith communities. Both will take as their starting point the principle that the family is the center of religious education and will see themselves as auxiliaries, *professional* auxiliaries, provided by the faith community to assist and guide parents. Schools will take a much more flexible approach to religious education (hopefully, to all forms of education) by adopting what is commonly called the open classroom, school without walls, etc. In short, they will strive to be much more *experiential,* directing students to available experiences related to faith life and providing these experiences in situations where families cannot. The school would have the further task, of course, of integrating the student's growing faith awareness into the insights gained in other disciplines. The CCD program, on the other hand, will find it necessary to schedule more serious and systematic study into the overall experiential curriculum, overcoming its image of "fun and games" or "watered-down religion."

Another shift that must occur, if the school and CCD are to survive, is in terms of their point of origin. Since both have the same historical roots and the same historical purpose, namely the intellectual dimension of faith-life, both over the years have organized their curriculum logically rather than psychologically. They tend to ask the question, "What is the most important truth in the faith?" instead of asking,"What is the most important truth of the faith for this age group?" We have seen that through much of grade school and to a certain degree continuing through high school, students are not ready for a logical presentation of some of our most basic and beautiful truths. So, while both the school and CCD have the task of providing a serious and systematic study of the faith that the students experience, this always must be provided *in keeping with the students' starting point.*

To say that CCD programs must provide their students with more of these opportunities for reflection doesn't mean they should introduce the mystery of the Trinity in its fullness by fourth grade, for example. It does mean that when a high school junior begins to ask serious questions, the teachers in a CCD program must be prepared to answer them. It seems an historical irony that we now provide more professional religion teachers in parochial grade schools, where they are not needed, than we do in high school CCD and adult programs, where they are needed desperately.

This leads to a final conclusion regarding the role and structure of the school and CCD in the future of religious education. If either is to survive, it will be only because they see themselves as partners in the same task, planning and sharing resources together (not just facilities but professional staff). Further, they must do so not just at the local parish level but on the diocesan level as well. The day when a diocese has a department of education (for schools) and a department of religious education (for CCD programs) is over. That such a division ever happened in the first place is one of the most disruptive and counter-productive historical errors in religious education.

In the context of the learning process and as a follow-up to what was just said regarding serious, systematic study, the *General Catechetical Directory* makes some very important distinctions that, properly understood, also will have real value for the structure of religious education in the future. In Chapter IV of Part Six, entitled "Catechetical Aids," the GCD lists *directories, programs, catechisms, textbooks,* and *audiovisual aids,* and makes some significant distinctions among them.

Directories (#117) are meant to promote and coordinate catechetical action within large geographic areas. They deal with general principles and guidelines suitable to a region or nation.

Programs (#118) are more specific, and the definition deserves to be quoted in full: "Programs set up educational goals to be attained according to the ages or places or set times, the methodological criteria to be used, and the content to be taught in catechesis. By all means care must be taken that the mysteries of faith to be believed by adults are already indicated in the programs for children and adolescents' catechisms in a way adapted to their age."

Catechisms (#119) are defined as having the following purpose: ". . . to provide under a form that is condensed and practical, the witnesses of revelation and of the Christian tradition as well as the chief principles which ought to be useful for catechetical activity, that is, for personal education in faith." The paragraph continues, explaining criteria and guidelines for formulating such catechisms. But the point to be stressed here is that catechisms are intended as source books for teachers to insure orthodoxy and comprehensiveness. They are not intended to be used as textbooks.

The *Directory* goes on in the next paragraph (#120) to define *textbooks* as ". . . aids offered to the Christian community that is engaged in catechesis." It then explains that such texts should contain an explanation of the message of salvation, psychological and pedagogical advice, and suggestions about methods. Much the same thing is said about audiovisuals (#122, 123, 124).

Note that programs by their nature deal with identifying the student's starting point and, consequently, the appropriate content and methodology for each age group. A program is basically an overall curriculum guide useful to parents and teachers as a broad framework within which to operate. Catechisms, on the other hand, are a resource for parents and teachers, a normative statement of the intellectual content of various truths of the faith. The program indicates what aspect of the faith the student is most likely to be ready to appreciate.

The catechism gives the parent and teacher an orthodox definition of the particular truths to insure fidelity to the Catholic tradition. Textbooks and related audiovisual aids are intended to provide practical implementation of both the program and the catechism. That is, a textbook should adopt the goals for each grade level as suggested by the program, recommend the methodology for reaching those goals, and provide an accurate (orthodox) statement of the catechism content, *adapted* to the readiness and capacity of the age group.

If these distinctions are respected in the future, several things will happen. First, programs or curriculum guides will accurately define student starting points. We no longer will have a curriculum developed from the logical presentation of catechisms. Rather, we will have realistic goals and methods for each age level in keeping with their starting point.

Second, approved catechisms will insure unity, as they should. But, viewed as a resource or reference rather than as a curriculum guide, their proper value will be restored. They provide a norm for what is taught; they are not intended to present the order in which truths of the faith are taught.

Third, we no longer will make unrealistic demands on textbook publishers. Until now, we have expected them to provide the overall program, include all the catechism, and also detail the practical suggestions for teaching. This is not the real task of textbook publishers. They should take the lead from those responsible for developing catechetical programs; they should remain faithful to the definitions presented in the catechisms. But their real task is implementation, applying the learning process to each age group, pointing out what are most likely to be significant experiences for that age group, suggesting ways to provide these significant experiences, offering appropriate methods for facilitating reflection and arriving at insights expressed in language the age group can grasp, and providing alternatives for assimilating these insights into the person's life.

The present confusion of roles between program, catechism, and textbook has made it impossible for publishers to fulfill their role and play their rightful part in religious education. When a diocese or parish views the textbook as the program, or views the textbook as the catechism, debate is bound to begin and division result. Each person will look for different things in the textbook. One will look for a logical presentation of doctrine; another will look for realistic goals and content in keeping with age group using the text. The first may praise the text because it contains an accurate statement of all the "catechism" he hopes to find. The second will reject the text, not because he disagrees with the "catechism" and its orthodoxy, but because he feels the material lacks the right content for the age group. In this situation, how can a textbook publisher win?

If, however, as the GCD suggests, the diocese or the parish *begins* by identifying the program, in keeping with the principles of the learning process, and then identifies a catechism or similar resource which it finds satisfactory, then everyone will approach the textbook with the same criterion: Does it adequately assist parents and teachers in implementing the program and introducing the proper elements of the catechism at each age level?

I predict we will begin to see more and more diocesan and regional catechetical programs developed, each adapted to the special needs and concerns of the Church in that location. Catechisms like the *Basic Teachings* will cease then to be a threat to religious educators, becoming instead a valuable resource and means for unity. Finally, we will begin to have textbooks that are truly aids to parents and teachers, since publishers can begin to do what they do best: concentrate on implementation rather than striving to be all things to all men. We might even see that happy day when particular publishers will concentrate on providing aids for particular regions of the country, rather than competing with one another for the national market. For example, a catechetical program for a diocese in the rural South will have unique characteristics not found in a similar program intended for the urban Northeast. A catechetical program for dioceses of the Southwest with their large Mexican-American populations necessarily will differ in important details from a similar program for dioceses in the Midwest. But the burden of developing specialized programs does not lie with the publishers, at least not initially. It lies with the professional religious educators who, by respecting the principles of the learning process, should begin to develop such regional programs to which the publishers can respond.

All this may seem far removed from the practical concerns of the average parent, classroom teacher, coordinator, or volunteer. In a sense, it is. But if the insights presented here are valid and become an integral part of the grassroots mentality, it won't be long before those in a position to develop such programs and influence publishers will be moved to act.

One final observation concerning textbooks. As the movement toward more parental teaching and family catechetics grows, we can expect publishers to respond to that movement in greater numbers. More importantly, we can expect them to develop materials that will better respect the interrelated roles of parent, teacher, and faith community. While materials presently available are encouraging, we hardly have dented the surface in meeting the needs of this most important trend in religious education.

For years, religious educators have been saying that adult education is our primary concern. There are sufficient statements in Church documents to justify the claim, and our analysis of the learning process offers further support. Yet, programs continue to be child-centered. Now, as we move more toward parental teaching and become concerned about faith communities, as we define more accurately the role of the professional catechist and the role and limits of the parochial school and CCD, as we better understand the stages of psychological development and how these affect what can and should be taught, we naturally move more and more toward focusing on adult education. First, in our concern for assisting parents, we logically will begin to spend as much if not more time with them as with children. Second, the necessity for forming faith communities directs us again to the adult members of the parish. Finally, since we now see that so much of the content of the faith requires intellectual and psychological maturity before it can be fully understood and appreciated, we again find it necessary to continue our religious education programs into adulthood rather than stopping at graduation. In fact, we are beginning to realize it is after a person reaches adulthood that religious education programs should be intensified. As the GCD states: "They (shepherds of souls) should also remember that catechesis for adults, since it deals with persons who are capable of an adherence (to the faith) that is fully responsible, must be considered *the* chief form of catechesis. All other forms, which are indeed always necessary, are in some way oriented to it" (#20). It seems safe to predict that as the above mentioned movements grow, adult education will in fact become *"the* chief form of catechetics."

Talk of long-range trends regarding parish structures, school and CCD programs, building the faith community, and developing better curriculums and textbooks may all seem outside the "real world" of the ordinary teacher or parish coordinator. Without authority and assistance to implement such ideals, knowledge of them can be very frustrating. While it is impossible to go into detail here regarding the what and how of implementing such efforts, we can at least end on a note of optimism.

Virtually every prediction made in this chapter is based to some degree on observation of actual efforts being made right now. Granted, such efforts now usually take the form of pilot projects or isolated efforts by more avant-garde parishes and groups. But momentum is growing. The ideas discussed in this chapter make up much of agenda at meetings of professional groups like the National Conference of

Diocesan Directors—CCD. Research and pilot projects in team ministry are multiplying in virtually every diocese of the country. Textbook publishers already have begun to turn more attention to developing material for special groups like the Spanish-speaking Americans.

So even if the individual teacher or coordinator is not presently in a position to initiate such programs himself, he can at least be comforted with the knowledge that much groundwork is being done. In short, help is on the way.

By way of conclusion it is only fair to say that knowledge of the learning process is not the cause for the catechetical trends we have been predicting. The trends are due to many forces. Adequate knowledge of the learning process will speed up these trends, though, since it both justifies them and makes them more understandable. Knowledge of the learning process, as stated in the first chapter, will not provide the panacea for all the ills and frustrations in contemporary religious education. But it may just be the missing link, the final piece in the puzzle that will enable us to synthesize and utilize effectively all the good work that has been done in religious education to this point.

bibliography

1. Regarding Starting Point

The following books can be used to supplement or document the material found at the end of Chapter Three. More important books have been marked with an asterisk (*).

Babin, Pierre, *Crisis of Faith,* Herder & Herder, N.Y.; 1963.

*Berridge, Sr. Dorothy, *The Religious Development of Children,* Cavendish Square, College, London; 1966.

Crow, L.D. and Crow, A., *Child Psychology,* Barnes and Noble, N.Y.; 1953.

Devlin, Wm. J., S.J., *Psychodynamics of Personality Development,* Alba House, N.Y.; 1964.

Erikson, Erik H., *Childhood and Society,* Norton, N.Y.; 1950.
*Erikson, Erik H., *Identity, Youth and Crisis,* Norton, N.Y.; 1968.
Ginott, Haim G., *Between Parent and Child,* Macmillan, N.Y.; 1968.

Ginott, Haim G., *Between Parent and Teenager,* Macmillan, N.Y.; 1969.

*Goldman, Ronald, *Readiness for Religion,* Seabury Press, N.Y.; 1965.
*Goldman, Ronald, *Religious Thinking from Childhood to Adolescence,* Seabury Press, N.Y.; 1964.

Group for the Advancement of Psychiatry, *Normal Adolescence,* Publications Office of GAP, N.Y.; 1968.

The Higher Institute of Catechetics of Nijmegen, Holland, *Making All Things New,* Divine Word Publications, Techny, Ill.; 1966.

Isaacs, Susan, *Intellectual Growth in Young Children,* Schocken Books, N.Y.; 1966.

Lee, R.S., *Your Growing Child and Religion,* Macmillan, N.Y.; 1963.

Mussen, Paul H., *The Psychological Development of the Child,* Prentice-Hall, Englewood Cliffs, N.J.; 1963.

O'Shaughnessy, Killgallon, and Weber, *The Child and the Christian Mystery,* Benziger Bros., N.Y.; 1965.

*Piaget, Jean, *The Moral Judgment of the Child,* Free Press, N.Y.; 1965.

2. Regarding Significant Experiences

Virtually anything can provide a significant experience. However, the following books provide the religion teacher with resources that have proven useful in religious education programs.

A. *Media*

The best single source book for finding useful audio-visual materials of all kinds is *Media for Christian Formation,* William A. Dalglish, Editor. Geo. A. Pflaum, Publisher, Dayton, Ohio, 1969. (Since the original publication, two addition volumes of resources have been published: Media II and Media III.)

B. *Structured Life Experiences*

This includes experience-oriented programs that can take place in an evening or a weekend. The following have proven successful:

1. *Serendipity Books,* written by Lyman Coleman and published by Word, Inc., Waco, Texas, includes a series of booklets centering around experiences and subsequent discussion and prayer. Most appropriate for older high school students and college-age persons.

2. *Faith Experiences,* published by the Diocese of Green Bay, Education Department, P.O. Box 186, Green Bay, Wisconsin 54305. Includes a program for freshmen, sophomores, juniors and seniors (h.s.) respectively to be used as an overnight or a weekend experience.

3. Two books by Tom Downs published by Ave Maria Press, Notre Dame, Indiana, can be helpful. The first, entitled *All Together Now,* gives a detailed explanation of how to provide a COR

weekend. The second, entitled *Strategies and Techniques for Religion Teachers,* centers around projects and similar activities that can be used effectively in religious education.

C. *Simulations and Related Activities*

While there are a number of packaged simulation games on the market, they tend to be expensive, especially considering their limited use. Therefore I recommend books describing such "games" as a starting point for teachers to begin developing their own:

1. *Structured Experiences for Human Relations Training,* (3 vols.) edited by J. William Pfeiffer and John E. Jones, University Assoc. Press, P.O. Box 615, Iowa City, Iowa 52240. Though not directly related to religious education, many of the exercises suggested can be used or adapted for use in religious education. Each volume also includes a bibliography of additional sources for such activities.

2. *Self-Awareness through Group Dynamics,* written by myself and published by Pflaum, includes a number of exercises that have been used effectively in religious education settings. Two other books, *XPAND* and *The Real Thing,* written by me and published by Ave Maria Press, Notre Dame, Indiana, also contain various exercises for use in religious education.

3. **Regarding Reflection**

Books related to facilitating reflection are numerous. I will mention some of the more valuable ones:

A. *Counselling and Related Forms of Dialogue*

1. Carl Roger's book, *Freedom to Learn,* provides an excellent overall philosophy of education

as it relates to establishing a healthy teacher-student dialogue. I can't recommend it too highly. It is published by Merrill.

2. The best seller *I'm OK, You're OK,* dealing with transactional analysis, can be very helpful to the teacher in this area. Written by Thomas A. Harris, it is published by Harper & Row.

3. In this same area I recommend *Parent Effectiveness Training* both for teachers and for parents. By Thomas Gordon, Wyden Press.

B. *Discussion*

1. The Serendipity Books provide some excellent ideas for stimulating and directing discussion.

2. *Group Discussion As Learning Process* by Elizabeth W. Flynn and John LaFaso includes a guidebook and a source book. Actually, it is intended as a text for training discussion leaders and as such becomes very technical. Published by Paulist Press, Paramus, N.J.

C. *Value Clarification*

The most noted author in this field remains Sidney Simon, together with his associates. His books, such as *Values and Teaching,* have had a tremendous influence on religious education in recent years.

Popularized adaptations of Simon's ideas abound and are now frequently found in teacher manuals accompanying various religion textbooks.

4. Regarding Assimilation

Since assimilation usually involves specific application of an ideal or insight to the concrete situation, it would be difficult to identify a particular book that would present those kinds of suggestions. However, most textbooks in religion do make suggestions for follow-up activities related to particular topics. Also it would be helpful for the coordinator or teacher to compile a list of the various service organizations, both church-related and civic, functioning in his area.

5. Regarding Trends for the Future

Precisely because we are dealing primarily with trends and pilot projects based on such trends, few books exist that present the "what and how." This kind of information is more often in journals dealing with religious education and pastoral ministry or makes up the content of talks and workshops at current religious education conventions. A few specific articles and books that further develop the ideas presented in Chapter Nine would include:

1. In the spring, 1973, issue of *Living Light* (Vol. 10, No. 1) a special feature entitled "Catechists: Their Ministry and Status" includes two articles dealing with the catechist's role in the future.

2. Two books that provide a broad overview of trends in religious education and their philosophical basis are *Lifelong Learning or Lifelong Schooling* by John Ohlinger and Colleen McCarthy, Publications in Continuing Education, Syracuse University, Syracuse, N.Y., 1971, and *Paolo Freire: A Revolutionary Dilemma for the Adult Educator*, edited by Stanley Grabowski, University Press, Syracuse, N.Y. The books deal primarily with the ideas of Ivan Illich and Paulo Freire, educational theorists who are having considerable influence on education structures today. 3. More directly related to the parish and providing more practical information is a book entitled *On Nurturing Christians* by Wayne Rood, Abingdon Press, N.Y., 1972.

starting points by age levels

birth to age three

FACTORS IN HUMAN DEVELOPMENT:

1. *Physical, emotional, and intellectual characteristics and needs*: The infant or small child needs an environment that stimulates him to gradually set himself apart from other persons and objects. Once he does this, he can learn to relate to the world around him.

The new-born infant is totally egocentric, aware only of what he feels. Consequently, he experiences other persons and the physical world only as an extension of himself. For example, if *he* is cold or wet, *everything* is cold or wet. As his experience grows he can gradually distinguish between himself and his mother, between himself and a mobile, between himself and a rattle. We purposely mention these three since they represent his three basic stimuli.

The mother's voice, her fondling, her warmth and softness and the food she provides meet the child's most basic need for safety and comfort. As he becomes aware that she is distinct from himself, he also makes a primitive judgment on the goodness or badness of the world. That judgment will depend on how well the mother meets his needs for security and physical comfort.

The mobile and rattle represent the infant's need for *color, movement* and *noise*. These continually draw the child out of himself and help him focus on the world around him. Without such stimulation, the child's development could be hindered considerably. Perhaps the most unpleasant sensation the infant can experience other than the physical discomfort of hunger or pain is the experience of boredom. Held prisoner by his initial inability to move about, he is forced to lie in one place. If he is not provided with colorful objects that move and make noise, he feels terribly bored—and alone. On the other hand, an infant can entertain himself for long periods simply by watching the movement of leaves on a tree outside his nursery window.

As mobility increases through crawling, standing and walking, the child becomes more capable of providing his own stimulation, though it remains necessary to continue to surround him with objects that will attract him. At this time not only color and noise are important, but also texture, composition, and moving parts, all of which present new stimulation.

The child enjoys feeling (and tasting) everything within reach.

Exploration gradually turns to the need for conquest. That is, it is no longer enough to see, hear or handle. The object must comply with the needs of the child. It must stay in place, open up, fit into another object. This calls for providing the child with educational toys such as blocks, stacking boxes, and simple objects that can be taken apart and put back together.

2. *Social characteristics and needs*: During this whole period of distinguishing objects from self, exploring them and gradually conquering them, the child needs the constant stimulation of *persons*. Persons obviously are more stimulating than any inanimate object. They talk, sing, and have moving parts like eyes, hands, and mouths. Persons, too are fun to explore and attempt to conquer. This is why it is important for parents and guardians to spend time with the infant or small child, talking to him, fondling him, and playing little games like "peekaboo." All these activities help the child to set himself apart from his environment, the first step toward personhood.

3. *Conditioning for moral development*: The infant or small child needs an environment that is safe and consistent. This insures that his first instinctive movement to explore the world and relate to others develops into the basic attitudes of trust and openness in his maturing years.

Characteristic of the infant or small child is his vulnerability. He exposes himself to the world in an uncritical manner. If he discovers that the world (and the people in it) repays him with discomfort, indifference, or rejection—or if he discovers that he cannot rely on that world to treat him consistently when he acts consistently—he gradually will develop a sense of fear and suspicion of that world. This forces him to retreat into himself and strongly affects what will be his adult attitude towards persons and his environment. For example, the infant consistently gets hungry. If his hunger is inconsistently satisfied, his capacity to trust his environment is impaired. The toddler consistently explores the objects about him. If he is allowed to play with daddy's newspaper one day and is punished the next day for the same action, he becomes confused and mistrustful.

Safety in this context means more than protection from physically dangerous objects like sharp tools or open stairwells. It is psychological safety, the experience of being loved and cared for, of being made to feel important. Symbolic of this kind of experience of safety is the mother who is somehow "always there" to kiss away a hurt, to rescue a toy that has fallen out of reach, to give a hug as she passes by. It is a pervading atmosphere in a family environment, one free of excessive strife and tension. Without this kind of environment and without adults to provide this feeling of security, the infant or small child cannot develop the trust needed for healthy adult relationships and the faith relationship with God.

4. *Intellectual growth*: By the time a child is three, he has acquired approximately fifty percent of all the skills and capacities of an adult. Eighty percent of all he will learn already has been acquired by the time he is six! Only abstract thinking remains to be mastered, and this will not take place for several more years. Most learning from that point on will be intellectual and represents about twenty percent of what man learns.

5. *Faith needs*: We have stated that physical and emotional development takes place quite naturally at predictable stages. It is perhaps more accurate to say that the natural life force that makes such growth

possible is active within the child from birth. Healthy growth will not take place, however, if the child is not loved by adults and stimulated by a suitable environment. Thus the role of parents and other adults who care for the child in the early stages of his development is two-fold: *to provide an emotional atmosphere of love and a physical environment that is both safe and stimulating.* In so doing they help shape the child's basic personality and establish the foundation upon which he later will build his religious faith. For this reason we maintain that the child's religion education begins at the moment of birth.

BASIC METHODOLOGY: No formal curriculum is proposed for this phase; however, the practices outlined below provide the parent with guidelines for the ongoing development of the infant and small child. These practices are:

1. *Adequate nourishment* for the child's growth and health; the prevention of physical illness through protective measures.

2 *A speaking social partner.* It is not likely that language can develop adequately if the infant is not spoken to. The speech of the adult is one of the principal ways through which information comes to the infant about himself and his world, what he is, how he feels, and what he is doing. It provides information about people, objects, and experiences he encounters.

3. *An atmosphere* that includes a reasonable amount of consistency and repetition. Quality and timing of care received from the familiar adults are involved in producing such a climate. The child needs significant periods of time when he is free from major discomfort and excessive tension and is able to give attention to people and things in his environment.

4. *Variety and contrast* within the atmosphere created by consistency and repetition. Variety and contrast tend to sharpen his perceptions and create in the child *minor* tension states that call for an adaptive response.

5. *Toys and other playthings.* Toys provide a variety of stimuli, challenges and satisfactions because of their structure, texture, color, configuration, and other physical qualities. Thereby they enhance perception and intellectual development.

6. *Physical handling* through holding, cuddling, bathing, lifting, and touching. The stimulation provided in this way is especially significant for the development of basic motor skills and for the development of a sense of loving trust.

7. *Opportunities to move about,* to play, and to utilize emerging skills and dispositions in a supportive and safe atmosphere. A combination of freedom and protection becomes increasingly important toward the end of the first year in the child's development toward *independence* and *self-determination.*

8. *Limits and prohibitions* appropriate to the age of the child. These support self-regulation and cooperative behavior from the child. The infant is born with the capacity to develop the ability to tolerate tension, to delay discharge of impulse, and to postpone gratification. These inhibitory mechanisms are a part of the infant's endowments, and their antecedents are seen from the early days onward. These capacities, however, are influenced in a very important way by the learning process and, of course, by the parents as the child's first educators. The process of socialization gives rise to tension and conflict within the child by requiring of him that he learn to adjust to some of the expectations and demands of society. Therefore, experiences of tension, inner conflicts, and frustrations are as essential to the de-

velopment of the child as are the experiences of gratification and comfort referred to previously.

Too many parents tend to protect children from conflict and controversy under the guise of letting children be children. This is unwise because children need to learn resolution of conflict early in life.

It should be noted that all of the above are more or less intuitively carried out and practiced by the normal parent. We have no intention here of relegating the delight of parenthood to a list of dry and calculated rules and regulations. Rather, it is hoped that such an objective treatment might clarify the characteristics and needs of the child during this phase, thus enlightening the parents and increasing their awareness of the wonder and delight of the small child.

preschool (3–5)

FACTORS IN HUMAN DEVELOPMENT:
By the time the child is three years old, he has succeeded in setting himself apart from other persons and his environment. He also has formed a basic attitude of trust or mistrust toward the world around him.

1. *Physical characteristics and needs:* The preschool child has increased his mobility through continued physical development resulting in greater coordination. He now can move about freely, exploring and discovering the world around him. It is essential that his early exploratory attempts are allowed and encouraged, with restrictions being limited to those necessary for the child's physical safety.
2. *Emotional characteristics and needs:* The pre-

school child retains the essential human needs of the infant and small child; he must be provided with an emotional atmosphere of love and security and a physical environment that is both safe and stimulating.

3. *Social characteristics and needs:* He must continue to develop the capacity to trust both himself and others, and this can be accomplished only through parents and other adults who pay attention to his needs and demonstrate in tangible ways affection, concern, and protection.

4. *Moral development:* Autonomy and rudimentary self-control are both important at this age. The parent can encourage this development by giving the child clear guidelines within which to operate. Within these guidelines, he must have sufficient freedom to exercise choices on his own. As was mentioned in a previous example, when it is time to go to bed, there should be no question about it even if he protests; however, he may be allowed to choose which story he would like read or which toy he can take to bed with him.

5. *Intellectual characteristics and needs:* As the child confronts his "new" world, he will attempt in a rather primitive manner to organize it, to make sense of it. This is reflected in his constant questions: "What's this? What's that?" His capacity for develpment of language skills increases rapidly in this context, and accurate names should be supplied for the many objects he confronts.

Essentially, then, the preschool child is an experimenter and explorer. His chief need over and above those of the infant is reasonable freedom to move out into his world, with the constant security of a parent who guides his exploration but does not hinder it through unnecessary restrictions. In a very real sense, the child's future intellectual development will depend on the degree to which his world is presented as an exciting challenge to know and conquer, rather than as a constant threat to his existence.

6. *Faith growth:* Trust, security, social stimulation, autonomy, and self-control are all important foundations for the growth of Christian faith.

METHODOLOGY: The guidelines that follow attempt to translate the theory given into positive and concrete action. They may be helpful for the parent or teacher in providing activities for the preschool child.

1. *Share personal interest* and delight in new experiences. Such enthusiasm encourages the child to discover on his own. Encourage frequent adult contact involving a relatively small number of adults.

2. *Provide a learning environment* that is both stimulating and responsive.

3. *Give prompt attention* to his needs so that the child is not overwhelmed by frustrations, but not such prompt or complete attention that budding attempts at self-gratification are extinguished.

4. *Provide a positive emotional climate* in which the child learns to trust others and himself.

5. *Provide an environment* containing a minimum of unnecessary restrictions on his early exploratory attempts, but a supply of natural restrictions that provide valuable guidelines in refining movements and actions. In order to create a safe environment for young children, many restrictions on freedom of movement are necessary. However, it is probably fair to claim that most environments go somewhat beyond the call of safety in maintaining such restrictions.

6. *Provide rich and varied cultural experiences.*

7. *Provide a physical environment* with a wide variety of sensory experience. Thus, in environmental planning, attempts should be made to provide various degrees of sensory experiences of color, shape,

texture, sound patterns, etc.

8. *Provide opportunity* for wide and varied play activities supported by an easy access to certain kinds of play materials. Play should be regarded not as an accident but as an essential function of childhood basically concerned with the adaptive process. It is related to that process that must continue throughout life and that profoundly affects man's ability to survive in his physical universe and ever-changing social environments.

9. *Introduce new experiences* that provide an appropriate match for the child's current intellectual level. Such a match is crucial for helping a child to move forward in his development. Learning experiences must not remain at the same level, nor can they afford to be too far ahead of the child's current capacity to learn.

grade one

FACTORS IN HUMAN DEVELOPMENT:

1. *Physical and emotional characteristics and needs:* The first grade child is active, changeable, emotionally responsive and highly imaginative. He loves to dramatize, to create, and to explore.

The child of six is apt to have frequent emotional explosions. He is excitable and tends to go to extremes of behavior. He has a limited ability to delay satisfaction of immediate needs. A correction, or a frustration he experiences from his own lack of skill in doing a job, or getting behind in a game, may trigger an outburst. His emotional responsiveness leads him to be quick to detect moods and emotional changes in the people around him. His quick and intense reactions often are distorted and may give rise to many fears, such as a fear of animals, the dark, or anything that may threaten him physically. He needs continual guidance and reassurance from the adult in order to learn how to handle his emotions in a healthy, self-actualizing manner.

2. *Social characteristics and needs:* In his relationships with others, he is egocentric. He has a great capacity to receive but little capacity to give. He expects and needs the adult to listen to him, to notice his accomplishments (no matter how small), and to encourage him in his learning efforts. Since his perception of the world is dominated by his own point of view, he has little ability to put himself in someone else's place. This renders him incapable of true dialogue with another. His conversations are monological and not dialogical. The average child of six has little or no capacity to empathize with the adult or to see the adult as having any value apart from his service value to him in meeting his needs.

3. *Moral characteristics and needs:* He tends to take rules as an absolute. He is not able to relativize them according to the changing circumstances of the individual situation. His motivation to follow these rules comes from a desire to win the approval of the parents for his behavior that they perceive as good. He avoids those actions that merit their disapproval. When parental love is present, the child's motivation to please through doing the "right" thing increases. In the absence of parental love, the child has no motivation to incorporate any "right" behavior. The closer the identification with the parent, the greater the child's desire grows to control his behavior.

4. *Intellectual characteristics and needs:* The six-year-old learns through concrete sense experiences and through active participation in learning

situations with concrete objects. He is not able to think abstractly or to understand and apply moral principles.

5. *Faith characteristics and needs:* He is sensitive to the world around him and open to spiritual realities. His spiritual development at this point must be seen in terms of his acquiring a "sense of the sacred," a real sense of wonder in regard to the world he encounters. He approaches life with a sense of surprise, delight and amazement. The child of six possesses an ability to marvel and to wonder. These abilities are very essential for acquiring a sense of God and they can be fostered best in an environment of emotional warmth and security. Through a secure climate, he is freed from inhibiting fears that would block the natural unfolding of his imaginative and creative powers.

Since the child of six needs and responds to the adult who cares for him and provides for his needs, he is quite capable of grasping the concept of fatherhood through his relationship with his own father. As he experiences the qualities of fatherhood in his own father, he is being prepared to understand the qualities of the Fatherhood of God. Through his relationship with his own father who cares, provides for his needs, and is faithful, he is preparing for an adult response of sonship to God the Father who cares, provides, and is faithful. Through his relationship with his mother, he is learning to trust that he is loved no matter how bad his behavior. As he responds through an increasing identification with each parent, he experiences his own growth in doing and acting in more other-centered ways. Through this deepening relationship between parent and child, the child's motivation to let go of his present stage of growth and to move into the next level of growth keeps increasing. On the other hand, when something goes wrong in this parent-child relationship and when the needs of the child are not met, the child literally refuses to grow. He refuses to function. He refuses to relate to others and to the world about him. He may refuse, either completely or to some degree, to develop his own abilities. He may respond through withdrawing into himself or through striking out in aggressive hostility to people and objects in the world about him.

METHODOLOGY: Many ideas about religion confuse the child of six, but these ideas provide a framework of meaning and cosmic security that the child of this age needs. Religion should be explained to the child of this age in artistic activities and at a feeling level. In this way ideas and images can remain fluid and open to the maturing process as the child develops. It is important that the child be approached on an affective rather than an intellectual level at this stage. The intellectual approach is incomprehensible and will merely reinforce crude ideas.

The most effective religion education at this age is mediated through worship. If the worship is expressed in the children's experience and language and linked visibly with basic needs, there is an exciting and rewarding field open to those teachers who attempt to re-think worship through the eyes and experiences of their children.

grade two

FACTORS IN HUMAN DEVELOPMENT:

1. *Emotional characteristics and needs:* Emotionally, the second-grade child is still quite vulnera-

ble. His emotions continue to be spontaneous. Though he is capable of exhibiting greater control than the preschool or first-grade child, he still tends to respond on either a totally positive or totally negative basis. The second grader remains quite dependent on his parents and has a continued need for tangible expressions of acceptance and warmth. These provide a response to his most basic need at this age, the need for a sense of belonging. If this is denied him, there is every possibility that he will experience emotional difficulties later. His capacity to share himself with others will be crippled.

2. *Social characteristics and needs:* The second grader is beginning to move away from his totally dependent relationship with his family. He begins to experience and identify with other adults (e.g., his teacher). Other adults take on significance in his life as important "bridges" to people outside the family. They are extremely important to him in the sense that they can provide him with the security he needs as he moves out "into the world." Relationships with his own peer group are a "touch and go" sort of thing. At this age level the child still is not able to relate too consistently with others in the group.

3. *Moral characteristics and needs:* The child at this age likes to have some type of structure from the adult. If the child does not have some type of consistent guidelines, his own anxieties are going to build an abnormal type of structure within himself. In other words, he will develop superstitions and all kinds of ritualistic behavior (like "knocking on wood") in order to protect himself from anxiety.

4. *Intellectual and social characteristics and needs:* His intellectual development is not ready for real interpersonal dialogue. His perceptions tend to be dominated by his own point of view. When this is the case, any dialogue or discussion is impossible be-

cause he is not able to let go of his own point of view and take on the point of view of another. He cannot consistently keep his own idea and make comparisons, although he may begin to be able to do this at the second-grade level.

5. *Faith characteristics and needs:* The second grader is nearing the stage where he can stand back, reflect, and absorb, although he has a short attention span. His spiritual needs center upon a sense of wonder and rudimentary contemplation. Secure and trusting relationships with parents and other adults continue to build important foundations for Christian faith.

METHODOLOGY: Life themes will involve children personally in what they learn. These themes are meant to be actively explored so that children at this age will know, either first-hand or by reflecting on home experiences, what is the meaning or significance of the theme in the setting of Christian belief. Take the theme of "bread." One could tell children stories about bread. Pictures and actual ingredients, such as flour and yeast could be used, showing them how bread is made. Seeing the teacher mix the ingredients and even make bread is one step better than being told about it. Even this is no substitute for the children making bread themselves. Also helpful are personal diaries, class workbooks, "show and tell," and exhibitions either in the classroom or in the hall.

Opportunities for spontaneous worship may arise in the classroom or at some quiet moment of wonder. These opportunities should be taken advantage of at that moment. While the theme of giving and receiving needs to be fostered in both second and third grades, it is important that the teacher note the difference in emphasis in these two grades. On the second-grade level, in keeping with the child's development, the emphasis is upon *receiving,* reflecting the fact that others love the child so much they give him all kinds of things. On the third-grade level, the emphasis is upon *giving* the reasons and the ways in which the child gives to others. His giving should be seen in relation to and modeled after those who have already shown their love for him by their own gift-giving; e.g., parents, relatives, etc.

grade three

FACTORS IN HUMAN DEVELOPMENT:

1. *Emotional characteristics and needs:* On the peer-group level, the third grader experiences the fear of being "left out," of not belonging, and the accompanying fear of not succeeding in school. This will become more pronounced later. Parental awareness of these fears and consequent reassurance are necessary.

2. *Social characteristics and needs:* The third grader continues the movement away from total dependence on his family. Though this is an indication of the development of a personal identity, the child remains ill at ease in his movement away from his source of stability. For this reason, tangible expressions of warmth and encouragement from adults retain their prominence in the emotional development of the child. It will not be until the intermediate level that he will develop solidified relationships with his peer group. Until then his groupings will be temporary and flexible, and parental guidance and support continues to be essential.

3. *Moral characteristics and needs:* Morally, the child at this age begins to internalize what were pre-

viously only rules and regulations enforced from "outside," from parents and other adult guardians. As a result he has an increased ability, though limited, to begin to set up *some* of his own rules and regulations. His peer group, particularly members of his or her own sex, will become increasingly influential in determining just what those rules will be. However, at this stage of his development, parents must continue providing restrictive measures. These should be tempered by an awareness of the child's increasing personal responsibility.

4. *Intellectual characteristics and needs:* Intellectually, the third grader begins to be able to see things from another's point of view, though not consistently. His capacity for identifying with another's thinking without sacrificing his own is certainly developing at this time. This is reflected tangibly in his increasing ability to talk *with* other persons, not simply to them, to engage in dialogue rather than monologue. His potential for increased personal involvement in learning situations grows accordingly.

5. *Faith characteristics and needs:* Faith and trust in significant adults (parents, teachers, adult relatives, etc.) must be nurtured. If the child's relationship with adults nourishes this faith and trust, and if the child grows in this attitude, a healthy preparation for faith in the Christian community and the official church will result.

METHODOLOGY: In keeping with the child's increased ability to intellectualize and participate in simple dialogue, special effort should be made to involve the child more personally in learning situations. He is now capable of writing simple hymns, prayers, poems, and stories. In addition, his initial movement into peer group relationships offers great possibilities for group activities, though care should be taken to keep such activities non-threatening.

121

Avoid those activities that would subject the child either to potential embarrassment or to ridicule from his or her peers.

While the theme of giving and receiving dominates both the second- and third-grade curriculum, it is important that the teacher note the difference in emphasis in these two grades. On the second-grade level, in keeping with the child's development, the emphasis is upon *receiving* reflecting the fact that others love the child so much they give him all kinds of things.

On the third-grade level the emphasis is upon *giving*—the reasons and the way in which the child gives to others. His giving should be seen in relation to and modeled after those who already have shown their love for him by their own gift-giving, e.g., parents, relatives, etc.

grade four

FACTORS IN HUMAN DEVELOPMENT:

1. *Physical and emotional characteristics and needs:* Physical growth is comparatively slow at this time, and emotional life is more stable than in previous years. In this grade, however, there is a marked separation of sex evident in interests, games, and activities. Because of his eagerness for objective facts, this is a good time to introduce basic sexual information.

2. *Social characteristics and needs:* Fourth grade is a transition year. The child is moving out of the close confines of family into a broader context of life. He has a growing capacity for self-motivation, re-

sponsibility, increased self-reliance. The fourth grader is group-oriented; he needs opportunities for group sharing, group competition, and cooperative effort. Acceptance, prestige, and responsibility within a group are significant needs at this time. A nine-year-old generally is dependable and loyal. He likes to be trusted.

3. *Moral characteristics and needs:* Rules and regulations become a part of his fact collection. He likes to apply them in his dealings with others. He is receptive in elementary ideas of justice, which are quite legalistic, and he wants others to act properly. There is a growing development of conscience and a desire for moral order. The nine-year-old likes to know where he stands and what he should do. A greater sensitivity to others is evident and fairness is very important.

Values for the nine-year-old take on a new dimension. He is beginning to realize that he must make some personal choices. He can reason in an elementary way about life-situations and can make his own decisions. There is a growing sense of responsibility and contribution to and from the group: family, peers, etc. He more readily can do things in a spirit of service, sharing himself as well as things, and he needs opportunities and activities in which this potential can be realized.

4. *Intellectual characteristics and needs:* He is developing the power to think and to reason for himself. He is beginning to exercise a degree of self-appraisal. His attention span is increasing, and his interests are broadening. The imaginative world of past years is giving way to a more real world, and he is eager to explore and to discover his environment. His thirst for knowledge is great; he likes to classify and to collect objective information, though still very much on a concrete level. This age is action-oriented,

interested in improving skills, and in testing abilities. Independent work now becomes more possible, if given adequate guidance and direction by the adult.

5. *Faith characteristics and needs:* His interest in the group opens the way for communal celebrations of reconciliation to the group. There is within the child a spontaneous impulse to seek reconciliation when he has been excluded from the group for violating its code, and also for the members of the group to readmit and accept back the repentant member, perhaps on stated conditions. This provides religious educators with an opportunity to make meaningful the corporate dimension of the Sacrament of Forgiveness. His preference for what is concrete and practical may make him overlook the spiritual. His prayer life will be more concerned with the realistic and will revolve around immediate needs and fears.

METHODOLOGY: The fourth grader's increased intellectual capabilities have obvious consequences in regard to teaching methods. Problem-solving situations can be very productive. His ability to classify and rank order items can be utilized, and memory games could be included. Because of his developing peer group orientation, a multitude of *non-threatening* group activities could be incorporated into a given class or session.

The child at this age is ready for a *very fundamental* introduction to the kind of book the Bible really is. However, the child's inability to understand time sequence, and consequently history, dictates that any detailed exploration of the Bible be held off until a later age when it will prove to be much more productive. The New Testament should be emphasized. Jesus is made real through instances in the Gospel that show him as human. Miracles and complicated parables should be avoided at this age.

grade five

FACTORS IN HUMAN DEVELOPMENT:

1. *Physical and emotional characteristics and needs:* Sex differences are pronounced in this grade, and this is a good time for ongoing sex education. Girls especially are approaching puberty, but boys as well as girls need objective preparation for the onset of this experience. This is a time when accurate terminology can replace infantile or even obscene expressions that the child may have acquired earlier. At this age also, there is a greater variation of maturity physically, emotionally, intellectually, and socially. Therefore, it is more difficult to meet personal needs.

2. *Social characteristics and needs:* The main frame of reference for the ten-year-old is his peer group. Through reading, television, and association with peers, he becomes increasingly independent of adult sources of information and of adult standards. The ten-year-old's attitudes are more flexible, and he is becoming aware of the individuality of others as well as of himself. He is receptive particularly to social information, to broadening ideas, and to prejudices. He can participate in elementary discussions of social problems, race, crime, relations of man to the world and to others. He has a fairly critical sense of justice and can make comparative judgments.

Talents declare themselves in the ten-year-old, especially in the creative areas. He has a special desire to be himself and to have his own originality. All his special skills, including those in interpersonal relationship, should be recognized and given opportunity for social expression. His behavior is more relaxed and casual, and he has attained greater self-possession than the nine-year-old.

3. *Moral characteristics and needs:* In moral development, there is a marked maturation. Although there is a certain propensity to moral order and "keeping the rules" with a great respect for law, his motives are more predominant now in assessing his responsibility for action. He begins to realize that intention is important in deciding whether an action is good or bad. His social world experiences are broadening, he is forced to make more decisions on his own. All this should be remembered as an added dimension in the preparation for the Sacrament of Forgiveness. Communal celebrations should remain the general form of the sacrament at this stage.

4. *Intellectual characteristics and needs:* Intellectually, he is characterized by an intense curiosity, a thirst for knowledge, and a desire to organize and correlate all the facts he collects. Because the youth's power of reasoning is fast developing, it is important that this factor be taken into consideration in his religious life as well as in his formal education in other areas.

5. *Faith characteristics and needs:* Consciousness of others should be utilized in clarifying—*on a simple level*—the meaning of Jesus, his message, and also sin. Opportunities for expressing concern for others also should be given (e.g., sending cards to shut-ins) in order that this basic attitude be nurtured and reinforced by tangible experiences. It should be remembered, however, that this concern for others is merely *beginning* to develop. The child should not be expected or forced to demonstrate it consistently and openly.

METHODOLOGY: The fifth-grade child exhibits an increased ability both to absorb material intelligently and to participate personally in the learning experience. The methodology utilized at this level must take *both* these capacities into consideration. There are basically three levels on which teaching occurs: the fact level, the inter-related facts and concept level, and the values level. The values level directly involves the child, stimulating reflection upon his own personal values. He is asked to confront issues. He will respond positively if the issues presented are relevant to his life. The values level of teaching is certainly the level on which real religious education must take place. The fifth grader for the most part is ready for such an approach. This does not mean that the teaching of facts and concepts be eliminated. Rather, these approaches should be combined with, but considered secondary to, the more personal and thus effective approach of actively involving the students in the learning process of value decision-making.

The Commandments should be presented as a beautiful plan of order. The child is legalistic. He should be helped to move beyond legalism to the spirit behind all laws.

Every effort should be made to encourage the child to participate personally in his own religion education. He should look up his own material, relate religion stories to his own experiences, and dramatize on tape recordings or film his own interpretations of what religion means to him or her. Students should express themselves in painting, drawing, sculpturing, creating models, writing diaries, making newspaper reports, and discussing that which relevantly engages their own authentic experience. In religion education, participation and discussion are absolutely essential.

A criticism that teachers often voice is that much less material is covered in this approach of activity by the child. This is an accurate observation, although it is not a valid criticism. If we are truly concerned for the quality, rather than quantity, of truth to be understood and desire that the child experience this truth, the time spent in activities that explore his experience is a solid educational investment. If desired, the activities could be done at home or in supplementary classes.

grade six

FACTORS IN HUMAN DEVELOPMENT:
This year is best described as a transitional year. It is the beginning of marked physical, intellectual, and emotional developments resulting from the onset of puberty. The girl normally will experience these changes sooner than the boy.

1. *Physical and emotional characteristics and needs:* During this year a person is conscious of the sexual development within himself and rightfully curious about the development and functions of the opposite sex. Negative attitudes and ignorance are the primary problems in psychosexual development at this age since the child does not yet really know or understand himself as a person.

2. *Social characteristics and needs:* Their involvement socially is primarily with "peer groups." Still during this phase, an individual acquires a greater independence and expresses this in his judgment.

3. *Moral characteristics and needs:* He needs freedom to be wrong and to make decisions. In the previous phase, a student was dependent on adults around him for the motivation to behave. In sixth grade, the child has the ability to assume more responsibility for his behavior. He will lack the perse-

verance to do many of the projects he tries, and while he excuses himself for these failures, he will be very hard on his peers who do not succeed in their efforts. Analyzing his own decisions and motives will help him build a Christian value system. Communal celebrations of forgiveness continue to be important.

4. *Intellectual characteristics and needs:* Now that the sixth grader can use his mind to a greater degree, he tends to be intellectual. He matures in his rational thinking and feels at home with abstract ideas. His scope of vision broadens, enabling him to make reasonable and critical choices. Whether he does this or not is another question. During this period there is an intellectual preoccupation with facts, reasons, and discovery through experimentation.

5. *Faith characteristics and needs:* His awareness of God still is rather vague. It is much easier for a sixth grader to understand and appreciate Jesus, the Man of Courage, the prophets of the Church, and the leaders of today who make our world a better world. He looks for models and images of what he wants to be. The child unconsciously molds himself to fit the patterns of heroic adults by recognizing what qualities he does not possess as yet. His self-identity and conscience formation are greatly influenced by those he admires.

METHODOLOGY: Remember that the young person is fascinated by the world around him, but he is beginning to be very critical in analyzing the facts and events presented to him. The history of the Church, the life of Jesus, the lives of great men and women of faith, all need to be presented in a dynamic way. A teacher must be informed about these men and events. The teacher also must be convinced of the importance of these people and be able to give young persons examples of how they are important in their own lives.

grade seven

FACTORS IN HUMAN DEVELOPMENT:

Life for the seventh grader is becoming more complicated because of new and varied experiences in rapid physical growth, psychological changes, and academic progress.

1. *Physical and emotional characteristics and needs:* Most of the boys now show evidence of puberty. The process of identity seeking intensifies for both sexes.

2. *Social characteristics and needs:* At this time, the young person's social involvement is predominantly with the peer group. It usually is much easier for the young person of this age to act within the shelter of the group. This allows him to go unnoticed. There is, however, a gradual acquisition of greater independence.

3. *Moral characteristics and needs:* He will notice the serious gap between moral conduct and Christian faith of the adult community. Consequently, he may rebel against all authority.

His physiological development causes conscience tension. His awareness of himself may cause him to engage in some sexual experimentation. The conscience tensions produced by his immature and natural attempts at self-expression are very painful. Unless properly guided, he may seek escape in spiritually and psychologically injurious defenses. With proper guidance, this normal situation of development can be a springboard towards Christian maturity. As he matures, he begins to make decisions for which he is morally accountable.

The importance of this year's instruction cannot be overstressed. It is of utmost urgency that the teacher recognize the crises and how important they are for personal development and Christian maturity. The instructor must create situations that motivate the student to discover and embrace basic principles. In this period he is forming values. He needs increasing opportunities for independent choices to form moral habits (i.e., to learn responsibility). Hopefully by the end of the year he will have taken one more step toward mature, responsible Christian living and will be prepared to admit mistakes and accept the Father's forgiveness of himself and others.

4. *Intellectual characteristics and needs:* He is learning to use both inductive and deductive reasoning. These new abilities can help him resolve conscience conflicts and pursue his newfound knowledge of what it means to be a human being. The wise teacher can help him use his new intellectual ability as a springboard to worthwhile personal advancement. The student can be helped to grapple with these new experiences as challenges that are a normal part of becoming real men and women. Because adolescents now are able to learn more about themselves and their personal and human needs, they are ready for a more mature approach to life, religion, and redemption. Indeed, this new maturation and this conflict of conscience and faith are opportunities to find out what life is really all about

5. *Faith characteristics and needs:* Spiritually, definite conflicts enter the adolescent's life. These are normal for his psychic and physical state. The area of religion is affected because of the youth's increasing desire for independence. There is a basic need for him to disagree with authority, so he rejects much of what is taught in the area of religion. More

than rejecting God or faith, he is rejecting adult authority. As mentioned previously, he now will reject many of his childhood notions of God. This is an opportunity to expose the adolescent to God as he really is. It is vitally important to work for basic attitudes towards life, God, people, etc. In other words, the realization that God is a loving Father, that he created all of us and thus we are truly brothers, and that care and concern for one another should be the foundation of our lives. Depth understanding and attitudes can be formed by working from life experiences to principles and back to the concrete for application.

METHODOLOGY: Since the purpose of the proclamation of the "Good News" is to give meaning to the everyday experiences of young persons, it must be done in a way that is relevant for them. Catechesis must help them answer the questions in their lives. Unless the "Good News" gives them some insights about how their lives relate to the rest of life, it will be meaningless. The approach of the teacher, as a result, essentially is a dialogue between the student's view of life and the teacher's faith vision.

It should be noted here that the seventh-grade student has developed a consciousness of time and thus a sense of history. As a result, an historical treatment of the "Good News" on a simple level is feasible now. Also, presentations or discussions on given themes now can take on an historical perspective.

Students will need the freedom to shift into independent action. Persons of this age need opportunities to plan, problem solve and discover. Team play will give them confidence in their abilities and yet allow them to remain anonymous within the group.

A teacher always must keep in mind that the child is just beginning to become a moral person during this phase. He needs a certain amount of freedom and experimentation to make mistakes. By giving him information and, more important, an example of Christian life, the teacher allows the young person to grow in a developmental way toward God.

grade eight

FACTORS IN HUMAN DEVELOPMENT:
Preoccupation of the sixth and seventh grader with the world around him fairly well describes the majority of eighth graders at the beginning of the year.

1. *Physical characteristics and needs:* Provided that there have been no serious psychological obstacles in the young person's life, physical, intellectual, and spiritual growth continues. These young persons are in puberty, and girls are about two years ahead of boys.

2. *Emotional characteristics and needs:* About the middle of eighth grade, young people begin to be more preoccupied with themselves rather than with the world outside. Soon there will be more important decisions that will affect their lives to a greater degree than in the past. The choice of a high school, a girl/boy friend, whether to participate in a sport, or even the clothes one wears will influence their relationship with others.

3. *Social characteristics and needs:* Personal relationships are a little more refined. "Gangs" still are very influential. The young person is hurt more deeply when personal relationships are broken off because he sees this as a failure on his part. As a result, some eighth graders become less expressive of feel-

ings. Being more self-conscious, some shy away from situations of risk.

4. *Moral characteristics and needs:* Life and one's place in it become a personal concern. There is a greater interest in knowing and experiencing truth. An eighth grader searches for the truth through experimentation. Unfortunately, in his desire to discover himself, he experiments in activities that can prevent him from discovering what he really wants to know: "Am I worth anything?" Faith vs. religion and personal experiences vs. learned principles conflicts are present still. Conflicts of conscience are strong still reflecting a still developing ability in the area of moral responsibility and decision making.

5. *Intellectual characteristics and needs:* See #4, grade 7.

6. *Faith characteristics and needs:* Students are at a stage of rejecting the religion that they accepted unquestioningly on authority in the past. Through the next few years they will be reevaluating and integrating a new set of values with which to direct their lives. Helping them through this period of needed growth can make them receptive to a meaningful relationship with the person of Jesus. This will happen if they see the good influence that Jesus has had in the teacher's life. An awareness of life in the Spirit has not yet arrived. But this is an age where explorations into the spiritual in a general sense can be exciting and stimulating for the young person. ESP, hypnosis, and related subjects fascinate him. All of these areas can be utilized in bringing the student to the awareness of that extra dimension in man, the dimension that ultimately puts us in contact with our God.

METHODOLOGY: The eighth grader's preoccupation with himself and his world, and his rather universal rejection of traditional religious values and teachings, make this year a very difficult but vitally important one in religion education. It is difficult because any attempt at teaching concepts associated with traditional religiosity will meet with probable rejection by students and with consequent failure of the program. It is a vital and essential year, however, for if the student is not exposed to new and relevant dimensions of the faith, there is the likelihood that his negativism will be long-lived. This year's content and methodology, therefore, must be centered around the acceptance of the student's basic negativism toward traditional religion as an opportunity to explore new dimensions of his life and the world. These dimensions at first glance may appear to be non-religious, but in fact they are stepping stones, bridges to a deeper understanding of the spiritual life that will lead the student to a later return to religious values. If properly approached, the student can grow through this period to what amounts to an initial understanding of real faith, not simply a return to what may have been for him a rigid following of rules and regulations.

Because of his concern for himself and his world, the eighth grader is open to presentations and discussions about topics *relevant* to both these areas of self and world. He will be responsive to topics dealing with "who he is" and "why he is." Treatment of various levels of his day-to-day experience would be productive. Discussions on what it means to be a person, on social issues in contemporary society, and on both historical and futuristic topics could be fruitful.

Numerous group activities should be incorporated into the program, though care must still be taken to avoid those activities that either threaten or cause embarrassment. The young person needs the freedom to "hide out" in the group if he so desires. Field trips are exciting for this age group. In regard to the content suggested, trips to planetariums and centers for scientific studies would be valuable and enjoyable. Any attempts to involve the student fully will prove beneficial for both teacher and student.

grade nine

FACTORS IN HUMAN DEVELOPMENT:
Adolescents can be characterized by two qualities. They are very conscious that they are no longer children. They are exploring an adult self-concept. By ninth grade, the emotional, physical, and intellectual changes brought about by puberty have resulted in very overt and contrasting differences between the boy and girl. The girl has developed at a more rapid pace than the boy on all levels. As a result, we feel that in our treatment of the freshman and sophomore student it would be reasonable to discuss the human characteristics of the boy and girl separately. *It should be noted well that these descriptions are generalizations, and as such should seldom, if ever, be applied without qualification to individual students.* By the junior year, the boy has "caught up" to the girl in his development, and distinctions on the developmental level will not be as noticeable.

Character sketch of the freshman boy:
1. *Physical characteristics and needs:* He may be in the final stages of puberty. If so, he will be struggling with awkwardness in a physical and emotional sense. He abounds in energy, and his life shows marked periods of happiness combined with frustration, due to a failure to accomplish his goals.
2. *Emotional and social characteristics and*

needs: He is self-conscious about his physical build and appearance. How he feels about his appearance will affect his behavior towards others. The ninth-grade boy may be courteous, but generally he tends to lack refinement in feelings. Due to sporadic bursts of growth, he is extremely awkward and uneasy. Because he still lacks any strong sense of "self," he will seek much support in groups or "gangs." Despite the great bravado he shows when with his peers, he generally is insecure and shy around girls.

3. *Moral characteristics and needs:* The freshman boy continues the discovery that there is something unique about himself. He is a somebody who can and must have values of his own.

4. *Intellectual characteristics and needs:* What he thinks becomes very important. To protect his independence of thought, he will react quickly to anyone who opposes his freedom to act in his own way. The urge to philosophize is building. His constant negating is clearing the way for philosophizing. He is discovering self by opposing. It is a negative discovery of self and personality. He doesn't want to be a carbon copy of someone else.

5. *Faith characteristics and needs:* His interest in religion revolves around a series of personal questions. Who am *I*? Where do *I* come from? What must *I* do? Does God exist and can *I* reach him? When can *I* be sure?

Characteristics of a freshman girl different from those listed for boys:

1. *Physical characteristics:* A girl is more advanced physically than a boy, which permits her to have a more developed self-image.

2. *Emotional characteristics:* She is more sensitive and more easily hurt or pleased by others' reactions.

3. *Social characteristics:* She is much more in-

terested in friendship and personal relationship than boys and more interested in people than things.

4. *Moral characteristics:* She can tend to a negative view of the life around her as she begins to formulate a set of values for herself.

Basic characteristics and needs for both the freshman boy and girl:

1. *Emotional and intellectual characteristics and needs:* Both freshman boy and girl need to grow out of the attitudes that are appropriate only to the world of children: complete dependence, irrationality and naivete.

2. *Social and moral characteristics and needs:* They need opportunities to express their ideas and to experiment freely. They should be allowed exposure to many experiences in order to give them a broad base on which to make judgments. In their attempt to evaluate their own worth and value, they need constant support, understanding and acceptance from adults. Such experiences are essential if they are to arrive at self-respect and respect for others.

The freshman needs to compare himself to convinced and committed adults, adults who stimulate him to reevaluate himself and his values. He also needs heroic figures, either from history or from contemporary society, who provide him with ideals to emulate. It is essential that adults compliment and praise the freshman for his achievements. This will help greatly in reinforcing the values that precipitated the achievements. In short, the freshman needs to be accepted as a person who is searching and growing, and supported by adults who show not only concern but understanding.

3. *Faith characteristics and needs:* The human Jesus, his strength and courage, can be of much interest to the young person of this age. Broad spiritual concepts generally are not attractive at this time.

METHODOLOGY: Avoid whatever would appear to be treating adolescents like children. The teacher also must avoid setting himself apart from them as a group in such a way that the group feels the need to oppose him.

The freshman demands fairness and honesty from adults. When teaching, stress rules of fair play, and be consistent in applying those rules. Use competition and games or contests to illustrate a point, but do not make these so threatening or humiliating to the "losers" that you magnify their already keen self-consciousness. Seldom put boys against girls at this age. Compliment achievements, praise generously, and do not overreact to failures and misbehavior. Set very concrete goals and outline in detail procedures for reaching them. Demand that they stay within the rules once they agree to the justice of the rules.

Approach Jesus through his humanity. The young person may be uninterested in worldwide spiritual concepts; however, it is likely that the humanity of Jesus and the way he lived it will be very appealing.

grade ten

FACTORS IN HUMAN DEVELOPMENT:
As explained in our treatment of grade nine, the more rapid development of the girl on the emotional, physical, and intellectual levels demands that we discuss the boy and girl separately at this age.

Character sketch of the sophomore boy:
1. *Physical characteristics:* The sophomore boy is entering into the preliminary phase of adult maturity.
2. *Emotional characteristics and needs:* His attitude at this time is typically one of disenchantment

with all that had meaning for him as a child. He can be extremely negative. This is evident in moods of deep depression, loneliness, and indifference to persons and things around him. Because the sophomore boy is easily bored, it is difficult to maintain his interest or loyalty. He leaves many projects and endeavors half finished. He can be physically listless and inactive, an apparent contradiction to his periodic hyperactivity.

3. *Social characteristics and needs:* Parents are predominant scapegoats for the youth's frustrations and confusion. Adults must be aware that the sophomore's criticism and contempt do not normally reflect a real aversion to them but rather are his way of expressing his own internal turmoil. Order has little or no value at this time, and as a result he is often unkempt and his room is chaotic.

4. *Moral characteristics and needs:* In order to escape the boredom common to this period, he *may* pick up some bad habits—drinking, vandalism, etc. These usually are outgrown as quickly as they appeared. The moral responsibility of the individual should be studied by the sophomore.

5. *Intellectual characteristics and needs:* He is capable of asking philosophical questions about himself and life. He may be capable of pursuing questions that involve the full range of abstract thinking. Though he is capable, chances are that he will not be emotionally ready to do so.

6. *Faith characteristics and needs:* His new insights into personal relationships prepare him for insights into personal faith and prayer.

Character sketch of the sophomore girl different from those listed for boys:

1. *General characteristics and needs:* Though the sophomore girl may exhibit many of the characteristics mentioned for the boy, she is more likely to have

entered into these characteristics during her freshman year.

2. *Emotional characteristics and needs:* She, like the boy, will seek meaning in life and relief from boredom by testing out new kinds of behavior. Although she usually maintains personal neatness, her room may be a disaster area. The sophomore girl is very susceptible to depression and being hurt. She feels more deeply and intensely than the boy, a trait that she will maintain into adulthood. Generally, she will emerge from this stage more quickly than the boy, but not without having experienced more intensely the loneliness and confusion of this age in her development.

METHODOLOGY: The best approach to this age group is one of practical problem solving. To this approach can be added that of the small-group format. This methodology is appropriate because the dominant characteristics of the tenth-grade students include their need to answer for themselves the kinds of questions they now are asking about life (e.g., What makes drugs wrong?) and their need to discover themselves in their relationships to others (e.g., Does Jim like me? Why? Why not?). A small-group discussion in which the students ask themselves, "Is it wrong to take drugs?" and in which they honestly tell each other how they feel about the question meets their need to come to grips with practical decisions they now face. Also, it gives them an opportunity to test out their own personality against that of others.

This emphasis on the practical and the interpersonal does not exclude the possibility for theory and formal input (e.g., the lecture method). In fact, this kind of input is necessary. But it should be realized that students will view presentations selectively and evaluate them in the framework of practical problems and personal experience.

The biggest mistake the teacher can make at this point is to assume an authoritarian role, expecting students to agree with his ideas. This does not mean the teacher cannot express his own deepest convictions and his own personal approaches to the life problems under discussion. In fact, this kind of honest witness to values is important. However, students must be allowed the time to reflect upon and to test out the values the teacher holds. This may take the student several years, not several days. The best approach for the teacher is to encourage students in their current interest and not be disappointed if they fail to maintain that interest. Avoid overreaction to their moods, and refrain from confrontation and debate. Remember that the sophomore student *is* learning, but in a negative manner. He must discover who he is *not* before arriving at the point where he can really discover who he is on a positive level.

grade eleven

FACTORS IN HUMAN DEVELOPMENT:

1. *Physical characteristics:* The young person of this age usually is mature and no longer undergoing significant glandular and hormonal development.

2. *Emotional characteristics and needs:* Ordinarily, the junior in high school has begun to feel more secure in terms of his own personality, though he still continues to test it. He feels secure in that he has escaped from childhood. In short, he feels he is beginning to possess himself. Now he begins to ask "Who am I?" and "What is life about?" in a more philosophical way rather than personal way. He be-

comes much more *intellectually* curious and critical. He asks bigger questions, and he seeks bigger answers.

3. *Social characteristics and needs:* The young person of this age usually is capable of sustaining interpersonal relationships on an increasingly altruistic basis.

4. *Faith and moral characteristics and needs:* This is a period of great potential and great growth, a critical period in terms of a youth's religious development. Not that the student will manifest externally religious behavior. Rather, the student for the first time in his life is beginning to ask authentically religious questions. At the same time, we must remember that a dominant characteristic of this entire phase is the need to test out, to experiment, to challenge, and to criticize. The student wants his decisions to be truly his own; this is one of his great psychological needs. So the teacher's main task is to supply raw material that the student can examine and digest. The teacher at this stage is not out to prove. Rather he is out to present. What he wants to present is the Christian interpretation of life. The student must be left free to decide for himself if he will embrace that life.

The student at this stage can be very demanding in his quest for absolutes and quick to demand a specific stand on an issue. He is also hypercritical of anything he feels is a compromise with the good, the true, or the beautiful. He is psychologically a revolutionary because he will not tolerate the imperfection he can detect in existing structures, including the church. This idealism should be nurtured. Time and the life experience will temper—hopefully not destroy—his zeal for perfection. He cannot understand yet how the "older generation" failed to take advantage of these possibilities, simply because he has not yet come to grips with his own limitations.

Religion education must not become defensive in the face of this critical attitude in the student. In fact, his fresh experience of being human can reawaken the teacher's enthusiasm. The most important qualities of teachers at this level are patience and humility: patience with the unfair criticism and humility in admitting that occasionally, perhaps often, the students are right.

The young person now has at least tentative answers about who he is personally. He wants to know who man is and what is mankind's destiny.

METHODOLOGY: The methodology at this level must be life-oriented: rooted in newspapers, movies, literature, social issues. It must be authoritative—as contrasted to authoritarian. This demands that the teacher take his own personal stand and reveal honestly and openly what he believes and what the church teaches. This means that the methodology must be dialectical, allowing for the students to react freely to whatever the teacher presents. In practical terms, this means that the best method is to pose the questions that the students are asking: "Why is evil?" "Who is God?" "What is man?" "Where is man going?" The teacher must pose these through contemporary media and contemporary experience: newspapers, films, literature, life events. The teacher must give his own answers and those of the church to these questions, and he must allow students freedom to criticize these answers. Finally, it is important that teacher and student engage in projects that give an experience of "doing" the Gospel.

grade twelve

FACTORS IN HUMAN DEVELOPMENT:

1. *Physical and emotional characteristics and needs:* Physically mature and no longer undergoing significant glandular and hormonal development, the young person is entering the peak period of his life in terms of energy, stamina, and coordination. The senior is psychologically and physically on the threshold of adulthood.

2. *Social characteristics and needs:* For him the basic question becomes, "What should I do with this self, with these talents, and these physical capacities I possess?" It is not always asked that clearly. We are speaking of a normative pattern rather than an absolute. Some seniors will not yet have developed to this point, *but the chief characteristic of the 12th-grade student will be concern for his personal future,* a future he wants to be both meaningful and satisfying. Two cultural influences are presently at work, however, that complicate this picture for the senior. First, though he is physically and emotionally ready to dedicate himself to a significant life task, he experiences at the same time the need for additional education if he is to be successful in terms of society's standards. This training may include six to eight years of additional schooling for some profession. With this comes the logical conclusion to postpone marriage and his continued economic dependence upon parents. Both tend to postpone the maturing processes and prolong the adolescent feeling of alienation from adult society and consequent irresponsibility toward its standards and values. For this reason, it is sometimes quite difficult to get the senior to take the ques-

tion of his personal future seriously. He sees that realistically he still has four to eight years to make up his mind. While boys experience this more keenly than girls, girls are not immune to it.

3. *Intellectual characteristics and needs:* By the time a person has reached his senior year in high school, he has gathered quite a bit of information about himself and has formed a rather clear though still tentative self-image. At the same time, he has gathered considerable experiential and theoretical information about life, the problems it encompasses, and the satisfaction it offers. His ability to think as an adult allows him to be profound, if he so chooses.

4. *Faith and moral characteristics and needs:* At this point in his development he is ready for a more mature commitment and a more mature self-direction in his life. However, he easily can revert to a kind of childhood aimlessness. This is not so much an indictment of youth as it is a symptom of a major cultural sickness in our society and in the entire Western world. There is a cultural influence that disrupts the normal development of seniors, namely the uncertainty about society's future and about the values that society presents to them. This is one of the major reasons why many seniors become drop-outs, runaways, or rebels, gravitating to one or another of the extreme cultural movements of today.

The senior *does* have the capacity and natural inclination to begin to make important decisions about the shape his adult life will take. But he is anxious in the face of the highly competitive and unstable society he must enter, and often he is frustrated with the fact that he may have to continue in the role of student and remain dependent for several more years.

METHODOLOGY: Be as personalistic as possible. Ideally, this would mean one-to-one counselling of each individual. This is obviously impossible in most cases. The division of students into small groups in an informal setting also is good, but it also may be impossible in many situations. Even when it is necessary to gather students into larger classes, the method can remain personalistic by making it as pragmatic as possible and by allowing as much room as possible for students to do individual projects and study. The students are asking personally significant questions, and they need answers that can be applied to them personally. Whatever method best insures this in your circumstances will be an effective method. This does not mean the teacher cannot provide theoretical input by means of lectures, films, required readings, etc., but such input, as much as possible, must be viewed by students as relating to their personal questions.

human development chart

The coordinator or teacher may want to familiarize himself with the entire chart. Special attention should be paid to the sections dealing with youth. The implications of this chart alter some of the former guidelines of curriculum development. However, the chart presents normative standards that must be applied with prudence to a particular individual.

Psychologists have identified characteristics of growth for each age and developmental stages that each person goes through during his life span. Both are shown on the chart. With this knowledge, the educator can provide learning experiences appropriate to the child's ability and his readiness to respond. For example, the average child of six or seven, according to the developmental norms, is not ready to grasp abstract moral principles for guiding his be-havior. Instead, he guides his behavior by following the example of an adult with whom he identifies, or he carries out specific directives assigned to him by the adult. Neither is the average six- or seven-year-old child able to make judgments about his actions based upon an understanding of how his actions affect his relationships with other people. Since his own needs and perceptions tend to dominate his thinking at this age, he has little understanding of the giving and sharing involved in human relationships. Grasping divine relationships in the Trinity would be even further above his ability.

Although this knowledge about the child at particular stages of his development is essential in order to provide appropriate learning experiences, an even more fundamental consideration is an awareness of the underlying forces within the child that either motivate him to actualize his potential or block him from doing so. For example, the average child at the age of two is capable of speaking short sentences, but he either may be slow in using this ability or he may fail to use it at all because there is no attraction outside of himself strong enough to move him to want to communicate with others. Or, the child of twelve may be capable of perceiving situations and events from the viewpoint of others while at the same time retaining his own viewpoint; but he may have no desire or enthusiasm to use this ability.

The child at any age level does not move automatically from one level of development to another. He either actively participates in his own environmental conditions or in a negative way fails to respond at all or fails to respond constructively. Understanding these underlying forces that motivate the child toward healthy or unhealthy patterns of behavior is equally as important as knowing what the average child is capable of doing at each age level. To assess this overall direction of positive or negative growth, the educator might ask such questions as: Is he developing healthy, self-actualizing patterns of behavior, or is he developing unhealthy, self-defeating patterns of behavior? Is he joyful and enthusiastic about life? Or is he apathetic? Is he growing in theological curiosity?

In addition to understanding the forces underlying behavior, the educator who uses the chart wisely should understand the uniqueness of each child. This uniqueness cannot be captured in any growth chart, which of necessity must give the common features of development for all children. He should understand, too, that within each age level there is a wide range of differences.